A COLLECTION OF PERFORMANCE TASKS AND RUBRICS:

MIDDLE SCHOOL MATHEMATICS

Charlotte Danielson

EYE ON EDUCATION
6 DEPOT WAY WEST, SUITE 106
LARCHMONT, NY 10538
(914) 833-0551 phone
(914) 833-0761 fax

Library of Congress Cataloging-in-Publication Data

Danielson, Charlotte.
    A collection of performance tasks and rubrics : middle school
mathematics / Charlotte Danielson.
        p.   cm.
    ISBN 1-883001-33-1
    1. Mathematics--Study and teaching (Secondary)--Evaluation.
I. Title.
QA11.D3454   1997
510'.71'2--dc21   96-53629
                                                        CIP

Published by Eye On Education

INNOVATIONS IN PARENT AND FAMILY INVOLVEMENT
by J. William Rioux and Nancy Berla

RESEARCH ON EDUCATIONAL INNOVATIONS
by Arthur K. Ellis and Jeffrey T. Fouts

RESEARCH ON SCHOOL RESTRUCTURING
by Arthur K. Ellis and Jeffrey T. Fouts

THE SCHOOL PORTFOLIO:
A COMPREHENSIVE FRAMEWORK FOR SCHOOL IMPROVEMENT
by Victoria L. Bernhardt

SCHOOLS FOR ALL LEARNERS: BEYOND THE BELL CURVE
by Renfro C. Manning

SCHOOL-TO-WORK
by Arnold H. Packer and Marion W. Pines

QUALITY AND EDUCATION: CRITICAL LINKAGES
by Betty L. McCormick

TRANSFORMING EDUCATION THROUGH TOTAL QUALITY
MANAGEMENT: A PRACTITIONER'S GUIDE
by Franklin P. Schargel

TEACHING AND LEARNING

BRINGING THE NCTM STANDARDS TO LIFE:
BEST PRACTICES FROM ELEMENTARY EDUCATORS
by Lisa B. Owen and Charles E. Lamb

THE EDUCATOR'S GUIDE TO IMPLEMENTING OUTCOMES
by William J. Smith

HANDBOOK OF EDUCATIONAL TERMS AND APPLICATIONS
by Arthur K. Ellis and Jeffrey T. Fouts

MATHEMATICS THE WRITE WAY:
ACTIVITIES FOR EVERY ELEMENTARY CLASSROOM
by Marilyn S. Neil

THE PERFORMANCE ASSESSMENT HANDBOOK
Volume 1 Portfolios and Socratic Seminars
Volume 2 Performances and Exhibitions
by Bil Johnson

TEACHING IN THE BLOCK: STRATEGIES FOR ENGAGING
ACTIVE LEARNER
by Robert Lynn Canady and Michael D. Rettig

ABOUT THE AUTHOR

Charlotte Danielson is President of Princeton Education Associates in Princeton, New Jersey and Senior Associate for Assessment for the Council for Basic Education in Washington, DC. She has worked as a consultant on performance assessment for numerous schools and school districts in the United States and overseas, and has designed materials and training programs for ASCD and ETS. Her work has encouraged assessment in the service of learning by both teachers and students. Recent publications include *Enhancing Professional Practice: A Framework for Teaching*, and the Professional Inquiry Kit *Teaching for Understanding*, both published by ASCD.

ACKNOWLEDGMENTS

The author would like to thank Leslie Abrutyn, Assistant Superintendent of the Penn Delco School District in Aston, Pennsylvania, for initiating the project that resulted in this book. Thanks are also due to Barbara Smith, Mathematics Supervisor of the Unionville-Chadds Ford School District and Donna Bucci of the Penn Delco School District. The author would also like to acknowledge Richard North, Mary LoScalzo, and Dino Ippolito of Hommocks Middle School of Larchmont, New York for contributing student work samples. Special thanks are also due to Bena Kallick for granting permission for reprinting several of the tasks, (with their accompanying student work) from *Exemplars*, RR 1, P.O. Box 7390, Underhill, VT 05489.

TABLE OF CONTENTS

FOREWORD

The *Curriculum and Evaluation Standards for School Mathematics* released by the National Council of Teachers of Mathematics (NCTM) have profoundly influenced the vision and practice of mathematics education. Through their call for a greater emphasis on problem solving, reasoning, and communications, the *Standards* have validated the expanded use of performance tasks for classroom instruction and assessment. Effective performance tasks call for such reasoning and communication by engaging students in applying mathematical concepts and skills in the context of "authentic" problems.

While educators generally understand and support the recommendations of NCTM to incorporate performance tasks for assessment purposes, a number of practical questions remain – how do teachers develop "authentic" tasks to assess students' understanding, reasoning and mathematical communications?; how does the use of performance tasks fit with more traditional forms of assessment in mathematics?; how do teachers evaluate student responses since performance tasks typically call for more than a single, correct answer?

Charlotte Danielson offers timely and practical answers in this readable guide to the development and use of performance tasks and rubrics in middle school classrooms. The book provides an excellent overview of the rationale for, and the strengths and limitations of, the use of performance tasks to assess student achievement and progress in mathematics. She offers a user-friendly, field-tested process for developing performance tasks and rubrics, along with practical advice for evaluating student work, selecting "anchors", and establishing performance standards. Finally, the sample tasks, rubrics and student work samples provide "tried and true" resources for immediate use, while serving as models to guide development of additional tasks and scoring tools.

Readers of *A Collection of Performance Tasks and Rubrics* will not be confronted with an "ivory tower" treatise on what should be. Rather, they will discover a valuable resource, grounded in the wisdom of years of experience in schools and classrooms, for making the NCTM vision come to life.

— Jay McTighe
Director, Maryland Assessment Consortium

PREFACE

Educators have recognized for some time the unique role of assessment in the classroom environment. Assessment provides valuable information for both teachers and students regarding how well everyone is doing. Students can see where they went wrong in their understanding; and teachers can determine whether a concept needs to be re-taught. This function, of monitoring progress on valued learning goals, is the first purpose of assessment, and one that supports every other purpose.

Assessment also defines what students must know and be able to do to succeed in a particular teacher's class; students frequently say that they don't know, until they have seen a teacher's first tests in the fall, just what that person values. Is this person a stickler for details? Or are the big ideas all that is important? When teachers coach their students in how to prepare for a test, they are conveying what is important, both to them and in the subject. Such coaching can serve a clarifying purpose for teachers as well as students; by specifying what their students should study in preparation for a test, and in designing that test, teachers must confront their subject and make decisions about what is truly important.

However, there is much more to assessment than simply monitoring of student progress and clarifying expectations. Because most tests "count," they motivate as well. That is, to the extent that tests or other assessments are used to calculate students' grades, students will try to do well. Tests can "count" for teachers as well. In some towns, for example, scores on standardized tests are published in the newspaper; student scores on AP tests are seen as reflections on their teachers' instructional skills; and some states and school districts use test scores as the basis for rewards or sanctions. When test scores matter, teachers will attempt to have their students do well. And while few teachers will engage in unethical practices, most teachers will provide instruction in such a manner as to assist their students in performing as well as they can.

But it is not only in defining the content that tests and other assessments influence practice. The form matters as well. That is, when students are asked on tests (and know in advance that they will be asked) to answer a number of multiple-choice or short-answer questions, they tend to prepare in that manner, committing to memory that which they predict will be on the test. If deeper understanding is not required for the test, they may not strive to achieve it. If a question is ambiguous, they will seek to "read the mind" of the teacher, to determine the right answer even if they believe another is better.

The form of assessments also affects teachers' practices. If a test does not require, or does not reward, understanding, why should teachers emphasize it in their own classrooms? If all that is needed in mathematics, for example, is for students to get the right answer (possibly without understanding why the procedure works) then the procedure is all that will be provided in some classrooms.

Assessments matter, therefore, both in what they assess and how they assess it. The content of a test affects what students study and teachers teach, and the form of the assessment affects how they approach the task. Teachers have discovered, for example, that if they want their students to become better writers, they must make good writing count in the classroom; they must teach it systematically and assess it authentically. A test of correcting errors, for example, will not do; they must assess students' actual writing. Similarly, if teachers want students to acquire skills in solving mathematical problems, or communicating their mathematical ideas, they must both teach and assess those skills.

These considerations have provided much of the energy behind the movement towards "performance assessment," that is, students actually creating or constructing an answer to a question. Teachers and policy-makers alike have discovered that when assessment tasks more accurately mirror the types of learning goals they have for students -- both in the content and the form of assessment -- the learning environment is transformed. The assessments themselves tend to be motivational and engaging; students invest energy in the tasks and commit to them. In addition, performance assessments even serve to educate as well as assess student learning; teachers find that their students learn from doing performance tasks.

However, performance assessment has one enormous drawback; it is time-consuming to do, both to design and to work into classroom instructional time. Even teachers who are committed to the practice of performance assessment find that they don't have time to design good performance tasks, to try them out with students, and perfect them for later use. Furthermore, most teachers did not learn to do design performance tasks and scoring rubrics as part of their professional preparation. And while many educators have learned such skills as part of their continuing professional growth, they may lack the confidence to use such performance tasks as a central part of their assessment plan.

This book is designed to address this need. It is based on the assumption that many educators are interested in incorporating performance assessment into their classroom routines, but have either not yet acquired the technical skill or do not have the time required to design them on their own. This book provides a collection of performance tasks and scoring rubrics for a number of topics in middle school mathematics, which teachers can use as is, or adapt for their students and their particular situation. It is intended to save time for busy educators, to provide examples of tested performance tasks. The samples of student work provide a range of responses, to clarify the tasks, and to anchor the points on the scoring rubrics.

Chapter One provides the reader with an introduction to performance assessment and how it is distinguished from traditional testing. Chapter Two offers a rationale for performance assessment, explaining its strengths (and its drawbacks) as compared with more traditional approaches. In Chapter Three the reader can find guidance in making an evaluation plan, and linking that plan to the overall approach to curriculum development. Chapter Four consists of an overview of evaluating complex performance, and includes a description of evaluating non-school (and yet complex) performance that can be used in a workshop setting to introduce educators to performance assessment. Chapters Five and Six offer a step-by-step procedure for creating a performance task and a rubric for classroom use, while Chapter Seven suggests techniques for adapting an existing performance task for use in one's own classroom. Chapter Eight is the heart of the collection, and offers performance tasks (some with samples of student work) and rubrics, covering the major topics in middle school mathematics, designed to be adapted, or used as is, in your classroom. The Appendix contains handouts of each of the 24 tasks which may be photocopied and distributed to students.

1

INTRODUCTION

This book concerns the classroom use of performance assessment, and the evaluation of student work in response to performance tasks. It contains a collection of performance tasks in middle school mathematics, but also includes guidance for educators to design or adapt performance tasks for their own use.

While performance assessment is essential to a well-rounded assessment plan, it should not be used exclusively. Traditional testing has an important role to play, particularly in assessing a large domain or evaluating student knowledge. But in assessing student understanding, in order to ascertain how well students can apply their knowledge, some type of performance assessment is essential.

In this book, performance assessment means any assessment of student learning that requires the evaluation of student writing, products, or behavior. That is, it includes all assessment with the exception of multiple choice, matching, or true/false testing. Classroom-based performance assessment includes all such assessment that occurs in the classroom and is evaluated by teachers as distinct from large-scale, state-wide performance testing programs.

Performance assessment is fundamentally criterion-referenced rather than norm-referenced. That is, teachers who adopt performance assessment are concerned with the degree to which students can demonstrate knowledge and skill in a certain field. They know what it means to demonstrate competence; the purpose of a performance assessment is to allow students to show what they can do. The criteria for evaluating performance are important; teachers use their professional judgment in establishing such criteria and defining levels of performance. And the standards they set for student performance are typically above that expected for minimal competency; they define accomplished performance.

Norm-referenced tests are less valuable to teachers than are performance assessments. True, teachers may learn what their students can do compared to other students of the same age. However, the items on the test may or may not reflect the curriculum of a given school or district; to the extent that these are different, the information provided may not be of value to the teacher. Moreover, the results of most standardized tests are not known for some time. Even for those items included in a school's curriculum, it does not help a teacher to know in June, that a student did not know, in April, a concept that was taught the previous November. Of what possible use is that information to the teacher in June? It may not even still be true. And even if true, the information comes too late to be useful.

In addition, the only way students demonstrate progress on a norm-referenced test is in comparison to other students. Progress *per se* is not shown as progress. That is, a student's standing may move from the 48th percentile to the 53rd percentile. However, the student may not have learned much but other students may have learned less! So while norm-referenced tests have their value, for example for large-scale program evaluation, they are of limited use to teachers who want to know what their students have learned. Performance assessment, then, is criterion-referenced. It reflects the curriculum goals of a teacher, school, or district, and when used in the context of classroom teaching, it informs instructional decisions. In the remaining sections of this chapter, the different uses and types of performance assessment are described.

SUMMARY

Classroom based performance assessment is criterion-referenced and is used to evaluate student learning on clearly identified instructional goals. As such, it should be designed to be of optimal usefulness to its different audiences: teachers, students, and parents.

THE USES OF CLASSROOM-BASED PERFORMANCE ASSESSMENT

Assessment of student learning in the classroom is done for many purposes and can serve many ends. When teachers design their assessment strategies, it is helpful to determine, at the outset, which of the many possible uses they have in mind. Some possibilities are described here.

INSTRUCTIONAL DECISION-MAKING

Many teachers discover, after they have taught a concept, that many students didn't "get it;" that, while they may have had looks of understanding on their faces, and may have participated in the instructional activities, they are unable to demonstrate the knowledge or understanding on their own.

This is important information for teachers to have, as they determine what to do next with a class, or even with a few students. They may decide that they must re-teach the concept, or create a different type of instructional activity. Alternatively, if only a few students lack understanding, a teacher might decide to work with them separately, or to design an activity which can be used for peer tutoring.

Whatever course of action a teacher decides upon, however, it is decided on the basis of information regarding student understanding. That implies that the assessment strategies used will reveal student understanding, or lack of it. And when used for instructional decision-making, it is the teacher alone who uses the information. The results of the assessment are not shared with students, nor are they used for grading. The assessment is solely for the teacher's benefit, to determine whether the instructional activities achieved their intended purpose.

FEEDBACK TO STUDENTS

Performance assessment, like any assessment, may also be used to provide feedback to students regarding their progress. Depending on how it is constructed, a performance task can let students know in which dimensions of performance they excel, and in which they need to devote additional energy. Such feedback is, by its nature, individualized; the feedback provided to one student will be very different from that provided to another if their performances are different. It is efficient for the teacher, however, since the important dimensions of performance have been identified beforehand.

COMMUNICATION WITH PARENTS

Actual student performance on well-designed tasks can provide parents with authentic evidence of their child's level of functioning. Many parents are skeptical of tests which they don't understand, and are not sure of the meaning of numbers, percentiles and scalene scores. But student answers to an open-ended question are easy to understand and can serve to demonstrate to parents the level of performance of their child. These samples of student work are highly beneficial for open house or parent conferences, to validate the judgments of the teacher.

Such indication of student performance is of particular importance if a teacher is concerned about a child and wants to persuade a parent that action is needed. It is impossible for parents, when confronted with the work of their own child, to question the commitment of the teacher in meeting that child's needs. Whether the work is exemplary and the teacher is recommending a more advanced placement, or the work reveals poor understanding, the actual samples of student performance is invaluable to a teacher in making a case for action.

SUMMATIVE EVALUATION OF STUDENT LEARNING

Like any assessment strategy, a performance assessment may be used to evaluate student learning and may contribute to decisions regarding grades. The issue of grading is complex and will be addressed more fully on page 19 of this book, but the results from performance tasks, like any assessment, can serve to substantiate a teacher's judgment in assigning a grade.

SUMMARY

Classroom-based assessment may be used for several different purposes. An overall assessment plan will take all desired purposes into account.

DIFFERENT TYPES OF CLASSROOM-BASED ASSESSMENT

Assessment takes many forms, depending on the types of instructional goals being assessed, and the use to which the assessment will be put. The major types are presented in table form, and are described below.

TESTS

Tests are listed as the first major column in Figure 1.1. They have always been (and will continue to be) an important method for ascertaining what students know and can do. When teachers decide to move to more authentic aspects of performance in order to evaluate student learning, they do not abandon tests. On the contrary, they use tests for those types of assessment for which they are well suited (for example, for sampling knowledge), recognizing their substantial strengths as a methodology.

Tests are generally given to students under what we call "testing conditions," that is, conditions that ensure that we are actually getting the authentic work of individuals and that the experience is the same for all students. Testing conditions are:

- *Limited time.* Generally speaking, time for a test is strictly limited. Students must complete the test within a certain amount of time (frequently a class period, but sometimes

Figure 1.1 Forms of Assessment

TEST		PRODUCT		BEHAVIOR	
Multiple Choice	Constructed Response	Written	Physical	Structured	Spontaneous

Adapted from a worksheet developed by the Maryland Assessment Consortium.

more or less than that.) This provision ensures that some students don't devote far greater time to the assignments than others.

- *Limited (or no) resources.* Although there are exceptions to this rule (such as open-book tests), students taking a test are usually not permitted to consult materials as they work. An insistence on no additional resources rules out, of course, trips to the library while taking a test. This provision ensures that what students produce on the test reflects only their own understanding.

- *No talking with peers or looking on others' papers.* When taking a test, it is important that students produce their own work. Unless teachers adhere to this condition, they are never sure whether what they receive from an individual student reflects that student's understanding, or that of his or her friends.

In addition, tests are of two basic types: Select and Constructed-response.

- *Multiple choice.* In a multiple-choice test, students select the best answer from those given. True/false and matching tests may also be included in this category. Short-answer items are technically constructed response items (since the student supplies the answer), but since there is generally a single right answer, such items are a special case, and share more characteristics in their scoring with multiple-choice items.

- *Constructed-response.* In a constructed-response test, students answer a question in their own words. Open-ended questions are constructed response, as are essay questions on a test.

Of course, a single test may contain a combination of multiple-choice and constructed-response items. In fact, most tests do; they generally consist of some multiple-choice, true/false, short-answer, or matching items for a portion of the test and several essays for the remainder. The balance between these different types of test items varies enormously, by subject, grade level, and the preference of the teacher.

PRODUCT

A product is any item produced by students which is evaluated according to established criteria. A product is a thing, a physical object, and is generally (but not always) produced by students outside of school time. Students may take as long as they want and need to, and may consult books and speak with other people. Products may be one of two types: written or physical.

- *Written products.* A written product may be a term paper, an essay for homework, a journal entry, a drama, or a lab report. It is anything written by students, but not under testing conditions.

- *Physical products.* A physical product may be, for example, a diorama, a science construction, a project in industrial arts, or a sculpture. Physical products are three-dimensional things, and take up space.

Some projects done by students represent a combination of written and physical products. For example, most science fair projects consist of a physical construction of some sort, combined with a written description of the scientific principles involved.

Products are a rich source of information for teachers in seeking to understand what their students know and can do. However, they have a significant disadvantage, which limits their usefulness for high-stakes assessment. This relates to authenticity. When a student turns in a project, the teacher has no way of knowing the degree to which the work reflects the student's own knowledge and understanding, and the degree to which the student's parents or older siblings might have assisted.

For instructional purposes, most teachers encourage their students to obtain as much help as they can get; students are bound to learn more from an assignment with the insights of additional people. However, for purposes of assessment we need to know what each student can do; this requirement limits the usefulness of out-of-class assignments for evaluation. When used, they should be supplemented by other sources of information (for example, an assignment given under testing conditions) of which the teacher can be sure of authorship.

BEHAVIOR

Lastly, students demonstrate their knowledge or skill through their behavior, and this behavior can be evaluated. Behavior is that aspect of student performance which leaves no trace; once completed, it is finished. However, behavior may be captured and stored, and then evaluated. For example, a skit may be videotaped, or a student reading aloud may be audiotaped. There are two types of behavior which may be used for evaluation:

- *Structured behavior.* In structured behavior, students are performing according to a pre-established framework. They may be staging a debate or a panel discussion. They may be giving a skit, performing a dance, or making a presentation. Teachers may be interviewing their students. Drama and speech classes depend on this type of performance to evaluate learning; it is useful in other fields as well. In virtually every state, acquiring a driver's license depends on successful performance behind the wheel.

- *Spontaneous behavior.* Students can also reveal their understanding through their spontaneous behavior. For example, their interaction when working on group projects, their questions during a discussion and their choices during free time, all demonstrate important aspects of their learning.

Because of the unstructured nature of spontaneous behavior, it is useful primarily as a supplemental form of assessment. However, for certain types of instructional goals, such as skill in collaboration, it may be the only appropriate form. The documentation of spontaneous behavior depends on careful observation. Many teachers use checklists so they can make their "kid watching" as systematic as possible.

SUMMARY

There are different types of classroom assessment. The major types include tests, products, and behavior. Depending on the types of instructional goals to be assessed, they are all valuable. For the purposes of this book all assessment except multiple-choice tests are considered performance assessment.

2

WHY PERFORMANCE ASSESSMENT?

It is clear that the design and implementation of performance assessment are far more time-consuming than the use of traditional tests. Why, one might ask, should a busy educator go to the trouble of changing? A good question, and one that deserves a thoughtful answer.

First, it should be made clear that when teachers use performance assessment, they don't stop using traditional forms of assessment. Tests will always be with us, and they should be. It is frequently important to ascertain what students know about a subject; alternatively, we must be sure that they have read an assignment. There is no substitute for a quiz or a test to ascertain these things. But as a steady diet, tests have serious limitations. These are described below.

THE LIMITATIONS OF TRADITIONAL TESTING

When we refer to "traditional testing" in this book, we mean multiple-choice, true/false, matching, or short-answer tests that teachers create or adapt for use in their classrooms. These are generally provided by the publishers of text programs, or have evolved over time. As noted above, they are useful for certain purposes (and they are certainly efficient to score), but when used exclusively, they have a negative influence.

VALIDITY

The most serious criticism of traditional tests is that the

range of student knowledge and skill that can be tested is extremely limited. Many aspects of understanding to which teachers and their communities are most committed simply don't lend themselves to multiple-choice assessment. To illustrate this point, it is helpful to identify the different categories of educational purposes (instructional goals) and to consider how they can be assessed.

There are, of course, many different ways to classify goals for this type of analysis; one comprehensive classification scheme is outlined below

- *Knowledge.* Most types of knowledge, whether procedural knowledge (i.e., how to wash lab equipment), conceptual understanding (i.e., the meaning of buoyancy), and the application of knowledge (i.e., determining the amount of paint needed to paint a room), may all be assessed through traditional means. Indeed, it is in the assessment of knowledge that traditional assessment rightfully exerts its strongest influence.

  Conceptual understanding, however, is not ideally suited to traditional testing since students can memorize, for example, a definition of "buoyancy" without really understanding it; their lack of understanding might not be revealed through a multiple-choice or matching test. It is only through their explanation of the concept in their own words, or their use of the concept in a problem that their understanding, or lack of it, is demonstrated.

- *Reasoning.* Traditional testing is poorly suited to the assessment of reasoning. While it is true that well-designed multiple-choice tests may be used to evaluate pure logic, most teachers without technical skills in this area are not advised to attempt it. Most of the reasoning we care about in schools (i.e., analyzing data, formulating and testing hypotheses, recognizing patterns) is better assessed through alternative means.

- *Communication.* In order to know whether students can

communicate, we must ask them to do so in writing or speaking. Attempts are made, of course, to evaluate students' understanding of written text and spoken language through multiple-choice tests. To some extent these attempts are successful but they rarely give teachers information they did not already have through more informal means. For the productive aspects of communication — writing and speaking — there is no substitute for students actually writing and speaking, and then evaluating their performance.

- *Skills.* Social skills and psychomotor skills are completely unsuited to traditional forms of assessment. A multiple-choice test on the rules of basketball does not tell a teacher whether or not a student can dribble. And a matching test on how to work in groups does not convey whether students have actually acquired skills in collaboration. Nothing short of observation will do, using a carefully prepared observation guide. To the extent that skills are important aspects of learning, teachers must employ non-traditional assessment methods.

- *Affective Areas.* As with skills, traditional testing is entirely unsuited to the assessment of the affective domain. To the extent that teachers attempt to cultivate students' productive dispositions towards work (e.g., an open mind, pride in a job well done) they must look for little indicators through student behavior. As teachers try to cultivate an aesthetic sense in their students, for example appreciation of the mood of a poem, or the elegance of a mathematical proof, they must look for little comments and signs from their students. Other aspects of the affective domain are equally ill-matched to traditional testing, from self-confidence, to traits such as honesty and respect for private property, through the ability to weigh ethical arguments.

As is evident from the descriptions above, if teachers use only traditional forms of assessment, they will be unable to assess many aspects (some would say the most important aspects) of student learning. Clearly, other methods such as constructed-response tests, projects, and behavior are needed. These alternative modes must therefore be designed and procedures developed for the evaluation of student work produced through these alternative means.

DESIGN ISSUES

Measurement experts argue that most aspects of student knowledge and skill may be assessed through well-designed multiple-choice tests. They point to well-known tests that evaluate problem-solving, reasoning, and data analysis. On further examination, by looking at the actual items, most teachers would probably agree that the items require some higher-level thinking on the part of students.

Teachers should not assume that, because such test items are possible to construct, that they themselves can construct them, or should want to spend the necessary time to do so. These test items are designed by measurement experts and are extensively field-tested to ensure that they are both valid and reliable. Neither of these conditions is available to most practicing educators, who have their next day's lessons to think about.

When teachers try to design their own multiple-choice tests, they encounter three related, though somewhat distinct, difficulties:

- *Ambiguity.* A major challenge confronting test developers is to create multiple-choice test items in which the wrong answers are plausible and yet, are unambiguously wrong. Ideally, the distracters (the wrong answers) should be incorrect in ways in which students' thinking is typically flawed, so a student's pattern of wrong answers may reveal diagnostic information.

  Such tests are very difficult to construct. Most teachers have had the experience of creating a test in which students can, by guessing or using a process of elimination, determine the right answer even when they know very little about the subject.

- *Authenticity.* In order to engage students in meaningful work, it is helpful for assessment to be as authentic as possible. Students are more likely to produce work of good quality if the questions seem plausible and worthwhile. But to design an authentic multiple-choice test, one that elicits the desired knowledge and skill, is very difficult. Highly authentic questions tend to be long and cumbersome, while more focused questions are often found to be boring and inauthentic by students.

- *Time.* Good multiple-choice questions require a great deal of time to create. And unless they are tested before being used, teachers cannot be sure that they are valid. That is, the question may be ambiguous, or several of the choices may be plausible. Hence, students are justified in challenging such questions and the evaluations based on them.

These factors, taken together, suggest that for teachers to attempt to create their own multiple-choice tests for complex learning is unlikely to be successful. Experts in test design can succeed more often than novices, but even experts are limited in what is possible through the technique.

INFLUENCE ON INSTRUCTION

Probably the most serious concern about the exclusive use of traditional testing relates to its effect on the instructional process. Since traditional tests are best suited to the assessment of low-level knowledge, such instructional goals are heavily represented (to the virtual exclusion of other, more complex, learning goals) in such tests.

It is well known that "what you test is what you get." Through our assessment methods we convey to students what is important to learn. And when the tests we give reflect only factual or procedural knowledge, we signal to students that such knowledge is more important than their ability to reason, to solve problems, to work together collaboratively, or to write effectively. Since multiple-choice tests are best at evaluating students' command of factual knowledge, many students equate school learning with trivial pursuit, and never realize that their teachers value the expression of their own ideas, a creative approach to problems, or the design of an imaginative experiment.

The most powerful means teachers have at their disposal for shifting the culture of their classrooms to one of significant work is to change their assessment methodologies. While traditional tests will always have a value, combining their use with alternative means sends an important signal to students regarding what sort of learning is valued in school. If good ideas and imaginative projects count, students will begin to shift their conceptions of the meaning of school.

SUMMARY

Traditional forms of assessment carry many disadvantages, which, when such tests are used exclusively, undermine the best intentions of teachers. These tests can evaluate only a narrow band of student learning and, even within that band, are extremely difficult to construct well.

THE BENEFITS OF PERFORMANCE ASSESSMENT

Many of the advantages of performance assessment are simply the reverse side of the limitations of traditional testing, namely, that they enable teachers to assess students in all those aspects of learning they value, in particular, writing and speaking, reasoning and problem solving, psychomotor and social skills, and the entire affective domain. However, there are many other benefits to be derived as well. These are described below.

CLARITY AS TO CRITERIA AND STANDARDS

When teachers use performance assessment, they discover that they must be extremely clear, both to themselves and to their students, as to the criteria they will use to evaluate student work, and the standard of performance they expect. For many teachers, this clarity is greater than that required for traditional testing, and requires that they give sustained thought to difficult questions such as "What do I really want my students to be able to do?" and "What is most important in this unit?" and "How good is good enough?"

These questions, while some of the most important that teachers ever consider, tend to be obscured by the pressure of daily work, and the normal routines of life in schools. The design of performance assessment tasks puts them at the center. Most teachers find that, while the questions are difficult to answer, their entire instructional program is greatly strengthened as a result.

PROFESSIONAL DIALOGUE ABOUT CRITERIA AND STANDARDS

If teachers create their performance assessments together, they must decide together how they will evaluate student work and what their standards will be. These are not easy discussions, but most teachers find them to be extremely valuable.

Occasionally, teachers find that their criteria for problem solving, for example, are very different from one another. One teacher may believe that the process used is more important than whether or not the answer is correct. Another may believe the reverse. They must resolve their differences in designing a problem-solving task, if they are to evaluate student work together. On the other hand, they could agree to disagree, and each use his or her own procedure. But the conversation will have been valuable in isolating such a fundamental difference in approach.

IMPROVED STUDENT WORK

Virtually all teachers report improved quality of student work when they begin using performance assessment. This is due, no doubt, to several factors:

- *Clarity as to criteria and standards.* Just as greater clarity as to criteria and standards is valuable to teachers and contributes to professional dialogue, it is essential for students. When students know what is expected, they are far more likely to be able to produce it than if they do not.

- *Greater confidence in work.* When students understand the criteria and standards to be used in evaluating their work, they can approach it with greater confidence. The criteria provide them with guidelines for their work and they can estimate the time required to produce work of good quality. All this tends to increase student engagement and pride in their work.

- *High expectations.* When they make the standards for exemplary performance clear to students, teachers are sending an important signal about their expectations. They are saying to students, in effect, "Here is how I define excellence. Anyone here can produce work of such quality by applying sufficient effort." This is a powerful message for students; it brings excellence within their reach.

- *Greater student engagement.* When students are involved in performance tasks, particularly those that are highly authentic, they are more likely to be highly motivated in their work than if they are answering trivial pursuit-type questions. As a consequence of this engagement, the quality of student work is generally high.

IMPROVED COMMUNICATION WITH PARENTS

Student work produced as part of a performance assessment is extremely meaningful to parents. If collected in a portfolio and used for parent conferences, these products can serve to document student learning (or its lack). If necessary, a student's work may be shown to parents next to that of another (anonymous) student, to illustrate differences in performance. Such documentation may be very helpful to teachers in persuading a parent of the need for additional educational services.

If student work as part of performance assessment is maintained in a portfolio, however, the selections should be made with care. There are many possible uses of a portfolio, and students can benefit from the reflection that accompanies their own selection of 'best work' entries. But as a documentation of student progress, items should be chosen that reflect student performance in all the important instructional goals. For example, if a math program consists of eight strands taught through 12 units, the selections made should document each of the units, and all the strands. These issues will be discussed more fully in Chapter III (Making an Evaluation Plan).

A WORD ABOUT GRADING

Many educators ask about converting the results of performance assessment to traditional grades. There are no easy answers to this question for the simple reason that the issue of grading does not lend itself to simplistic approaches. The reasons for this difficulty, however, are not related to performance assessment, but to the varied methods and purposes for assigning grades.

A "score" on a performance assessment is a straightforward matter; student work is evaluated against a clear standard and a judgment made as to where it stands against that standard. If students' grades are also intended (solely) to reflect the degree of mastery of the curriculum, then the score on the performance assessment can be translated in a fairly linear way to a grade. A score of "4" could be an "A," a "3" could be a "B" and so forth.

However, there are several reasons why such a procedure may not be ideal. For one thing, most teachers use other methods in addition to performance tasks to assess student learning. The typical evaluation plan used by a teacher will include tests as well as performance items. Therefore, the results from different methods must be combined in some manner, including weighting some items more than others.

In addition, many teachers incorporate other elements in addition to achievement against a standard into a grade. They may want to build in the degree of progress from earlier work, for example, or the amount of effort or discipline displayed by a student. Alternatively, teachers may have offered some students a lot of coaching in their performance assessments (thereby using them also as teaching tools) and they may recognize that the students' performance reflects more than what they could do on their own.

Therefore, while performance assessments may not translate directly into grades, it may be a good idea to establish some connection between them, making the necessary provision for combining scores on different assessments. If this is done, it sends powerful messages to students. Primarily, such a procedure takes the mystery out of grading, and allows students to know in advance the criteria by which their work will be evaluated. In addition, it also conveys to students that high grades are within the reach of all students. Over time they recognize that if they work hard, they (all of them) can do well. In this situation, good grades are not rationed; all students whose work is at the highest standard can get an "A." As students come to internalize this awareness, and act upon it, it can transform a classroom into a far more purposeful place, and one in which students are concerned with the quality of their work.

SUMMARY

The use of performance assessment conributes many important benefits, beyond strictly measurement issues, to the culture of a classroom. These advantages are derived from clarity of criteria and standards, and benefit teachers, students, and parents.

3

MAKING AN
EVALUATION PLAN

Designing and implementing performance assessment entails a major investment of time and energy. In order to ensure that this investment is a wise one, and yields the desired benefits, it is essential to work from a plan. How to develop such a plan, and coordinate it with a school or district's curriculum, is the subject of this chapter.

A CURRICULUM MAP

A useful approach to developing an assessment plan for mathematics instruction is to begin with a consideration of goals in the mathematics curriculum as a whole. An assessment plan, after all, should have as its goal the assessment of student learning in the curriculum; it makes no sense in isolation from that curriculum. Therefore, a plan for assessment should be created with the whole curriculum in mind.

MAJOR OUTCOMES, GOALS, OR STRANDS

A good place to start in thinking about the assessment demands of the curriculum is to consider the curriculum's major outcomes, goals, or strands. Most listings of major mathematics outcomes, or listings of mathematics goals by strand are organized, at least loosely, around the standards published by the National Council of Teachers of Mathematics (NCTM) in 1989. These standards have had an enormous and positive influence on the teaching of mathematics, and have caused educators everywhere to think more deeply about what they teach and how to engage their students in conceptual understanding. The NCTM standards are organized in 13 major areas:

- mathematics as problem solving
- mathematics as communication
- mathematics as reasoning
- mathematical connections
- numbers and number relationships
- number systems and number theory
- computation and estimation
- patterns and functions
- algebra
- statistics
- probability
- geometry
- measurement

Most schools and districts now use some variation on the NCTM Standards to organize their mathematics curriculum into major strands, or around major outcomes. Naturally, the numbers and number relationships, for example, taught in the second grade are very different from those in eighth grade but the concept is addressed at both levels. The strands provide the unifying themes that are carried through the entire mathematics program.

Some states, through the State Department of Education, have mandated (or highly recommended) mathematics goals or outcomes also derived from the NCTM *Standards.* For example, Pennsylvania has identified seven major mathematics outcomes. These are, briefly:

- numbers and number systems
- estimation, computation, and measurement with the appropriate use of technology
- patterns, functions, and relations
- formulating and solving problems and communicating the results

- algebra and geometry
- charts, tables and graphs
- statistics and probability

Other states, for example California, have also identified major mathematics outcomes, or strands. Local districts then base their broad goals for mathematics education on those they receive from their state. For example, the Norfolk, Virginia, public schools specify the following:

- computation
- estimation
- organizing data
- analyzing problems
- formulating conclusions
- determining logical solutions

These broad goals, outcomes, or strands provide the framework for curriculum planning. They do not comprise a curriculum; that is developed from the outcomes for each grade level. But they do offer guidance for those preparing the curriculum at each stage.

TOPICS OR UNITS

What students work on every day, and the way in which most mathematics textbooks are organized, is a series of topics or units, rather than outcomes or strands. For example, in a typical seventh grade mathematics text, the chapters concern:

- addition and subtraction expressions
- multiplication and division expressions
- multiplication and division of decimals
- graphing and statistics
- geometry and measurement
- addition and subtraction of fractions
- multiplication and division of fractions
- integers and rational numbers
- ratio, proportion, and percent
- geometry

- area and volume
- algebra and coordinate geometry
- probability

Clearly, some of the topics fit well with some of the strands. For example, the concepts taught in the "geometry" chapter would address the goals in the "geometry" strand. But some of the other connections are not nearly so obvious. In which chapter, for instance, would one find material related to "mathematics as communication," or "estimation?" If educators are committed to addressing all the goals stated or implied in the NCTM *Standards*, or the equivalent document from their own state or district, then they must match the topics or units they teach with the goals inherent in those standards. The best technique to use for this purpose is a matrix, which is described in the next section. A sample matrix is presented on the next page. (Figure 3.1)

CREATING THE CURRICULUM MAP

Across the top of the matrix are listed all the strands, major goals, or outcomes of the mathematics program. In the matrix provided, the ones listed are those developed by the New Standards Project. Down the left-hand side are listed all the topics or units in the year's curriculum, organized, insofar as can be known, in sequence. Then, for each unit or topic, teachers should consider which of the strands or outcomes the topic addresses, and place an X in the corresponding box.

In some cases, research is needed in order to know where to place the X's. For example, if one of the major strands is estimation, many topics may be used to develop that skill, but some are probably better than others; estimation is probably better suited as a component of computation than of geometry. Furthermore, some textbooks will develop the skill of estimation in the context of one topic, others in another. It may be an empirical question then, which topics may be used to develop which of the outcomes, and can be determined by examining the text in use.

What results from this process is a map of the curriculum,

FIGURE 3.1 CURRICULUM/ASSESSMENT PLANNING GUIDE
MATHEMATICS

Course/Grade _____

Outcomes / Units or Topics	Numbers and Number Systems	Computation Measurement Estimation & Technology	Patterns Functions Relations	Formulate & Solve Problems; Communicate	Algebra Geometry Probability Statistics	Charts Tables Graphs	Statistics Probability

demonstrating the ways in which the different strands or outcomes are (or can be, given the textbook in use) addressed in each of the topics of the curriculum. No doubt some strands receive heavier emphasis than others. In most texts, for example, "computation" is much more heavily weighed than "patterns and functions."

If the map reveals large gaps in the curriculum, for example, if the curriculum map shows that some of the outcomes are not adequately addressed by the program in use, then some adjustments must be made. It is possible that a given curriculum lacks focus on an entire strand of the NCTM standards e.g., mathematical communication. In that case, educators will have to determine in which topics they could develop that skill. Once determined, they can then add X's to the appropriate boxes. For instance, they could decide to add, to each of their units, an objective and the corresponding instructional activities addressing the issue of student communication of the ideas of the unit, whether it is addition of fractions or measurement. In that way, they would adequately address all the different Standards.

SUMMARY

A curriculum map can be used to define which units or topics in a curriculum may be used to help students acquire the knowledge and skills inherent in a state's mathematics framework. The map is created by local educators, using the appropriate framework and their own textbook, through the exercise of professional judgment.

ASSESSMENT METHODOLOGIES

Once the curriculum map has been produced, educators must determine how each of the outcomes and each of the topics, are to be assessed. Some will lend themselves to traditional testing while others will require more complex performance assessment.

THE ROLE OF TRADITIONAL TESTING

Many mathematics curriculum goals may be assessed through traditional testing. It is, and will always be, important for students to be able to perform accurate computations, to factor polynomials, and to execute a geometric proof. The correct use of algorithms is an important part of mathematical literacy. For all these reasons, educators would be ill-advised to abandon the use of traditional tests as part of their total assessment plan.

However, traditional testing is limited in what it can achieve. As teachers survey the curriculum map they have produced, they discover that some of the X's they have written simply do not lend themselves to a multiple-choice or short-answer test. What kind of test, for example, could one construct that would assess students on the communication of ideas in statistics? Or on the use of patterns and functions to solve problems in geometry?

Moreover, many educators argue that the use of traditional tests, even in those areas of the curriculum where they would appear to be best suited, can do actual harm. This relates to the fact that some students, and their teachers, confuse procedural knowledge with conceptual understanding. That is, students learn a procedure, an algorithm, for getting "the right answer" with little or no understanding of how or why the procedure works, where it would be useful, or what the algorithm accomplishes. Therefore, they can take a test and solve problems correctly, with poor conceptual understanding. If the assessment procedures used do not reveal that lack of understanding, the students may move along to more complex concepts, ones that build on the previous ones, with an increasingly shaky foundation.

Therefore, while traditional tests may be highly useful in assessing certain aspects of the mathematics curriculum, they should be used with caution, and with full awareness of their limitations.

THE PLACE FOR PERFORMANCE ASSESSMENT

Performance assessment is the technique of choice for evaluating student understanding of much of the mathematics curriculum. When students are asked to complete a task, or when they are asked to explain their thinking, they reveal their understanding of complex topics.

Sometimes performance assessment in mathematics can consist of a small addition to traditional testing. For example, students might be asked to solve a fairly traditional problem, but then be asked to explain why they selected the approach they did. Their explanation will reveal their understanding of the process, or their lack of it, and will also serve to assess their skill in the communication of mathematical ideas.

In addition, the authentic application of mathematical procedures is highly motivational to students. Many students regard the applications problems (word problems) they encounter in most mathematics textbooks with disbelief; their reaction is frequently one of 'who cares?' However, with some thought, most teachers are able to create situations that students in their classes might actually encounter, which require the application of the mathematical ideas included in a given unit. The creation of such a task is the subject of Chapter 5, while the adaptation of an existing task is considered in Chapter 7.

A PLAN TO GET STARTED

The idea of creating (or even adapting) performance tasks for all those areas of the mathematics curriculum for which they would be well suited can be a daunting one. After all, if students as well as teachers are unfamiliar with such an approach it is likely to take more time than planned. And since it is unfamiliar, everyone involved is likely to encounter unexpected difficulties. How, then, should one begin?

In general, one should start small. Once the techniques and practices of performance assessment are well understood, and once teachers and students both have some experience in the methodology, performance tasks may be used frequently, particularly if they are small ones. However, when just beginning, it is recommended that teachers use performance tasks only infrequently, at a rate of 4-6 per year. Such a schedule permits teachers the time to create or adapt their tasks and ensure that they will accomplish their desired purposes, and to evaluate student work carefully. If only one or two tasks per quarter are administered, then they should be those that have the promise to reveal the maximum information about student understanding.

Once teachers have acquired experience in the use of performance tasks, they may want to use them more frequently and more informally. However, even with experience, few teachers will administer more than two or three such tasks per month.

SUMMARY

Based on the curriculum map, educators can create an evaluation plan. This plan will include both traditional testing and performance assessment. As they move to performance assessment, teachers are advised to start small.

4

EVALUATING COMPLEX PERFORMANCE

The major advantage of multiple-choice, matching and true/false tests concerns the ease of scoring them; it does not take long to mark an answer "right" or "wrong." Indeed, this speed and ease of correction is their primary value in large-scale testing programs. Because standardized tests are machine-scorable and consequently, inexpensive to administer, they can provide large amounts of data cheaply to school districts and states.

A student's performance on a multiple-choice or short-answer test may be described in terms of percentages. One student might score 87%, another 94%, still another 68%. But when teachers use other assessment methodologies, the concept of "percent correct" loses much of its meaning. What is 87% of an essay? How good (and in what way) should a skit be to receive a score of 94%?

These are not simple questions, and their answers constitute the heart of performance assessment. But there are answers, and answers that respect the important measurement principles of equity, validity, and reliability. This section, through a non-school example, introduces the techniques of evaluating performance, and then discusses each of the issues raised.

A NON-SCHOOL EXAMPLE

All the principles involved in the evaluation of complex performance may be illustrated by an everyday example: that of going to a restaurant. By reading through this example, readers will address, in a familiar form, all the issues they will encounter in designing systems of performance assessment for classroom use. Moreover, it will be evident that the methods for evaluating performance reflect, at their heart, only common sense.

THE SITUATION

Let's imagine that we are opening a restaurant in your town, and that we are at the point of hiring waiters and waitresses. We know that it is important that the waiters and waitresses be skilled, so we want to hire the best we can find. As part of our search, we have decided to eat in some restaurants already in existence, to see if there are people working in these establishments that we can lure away to our restaurant. Consequently, we are preparing to embark on our search mission.

THE CRITERIA

How will we know what to look for? We must determine the five or six most important qualities we would watch for in a good waiter or waitress. But since our focus here is on "performance," we should list only those qualities that are visible to a customer (such as appearance), and not other qualities which, while they might be important to an employer (such as getting to work on time) are not seen by a customer.

A reasonable list of criteria will include such qualities as: Courtesy, Appearance, Responsiveness, Knowledge, Coordination, Accuracy. It is important to write the criteria using neutral, rather than positive, words. That is, for reasons that will soon become apparent, we should write "appearance" rather than "neat."

These criteria could become, of course, a checklist. That is, we could eat in a restaurant and determine whether our server was courteous, responsive, or knowledgeable, etc. We could answer each of the items with a "yes" or "no," and then count the "yes'es." However, life tends to be more complicated than a checklist. That is, a waiter or waitresss is somewhat knowledgeable, mostly accurate, a little bit coordinated.

How do we accommodate these degrees of performance? How can we design a system that respects the complexity of the performance, and which we can use to actually compare two or more individuals? The answer is to create a "rubric," a scoring guide.

THE SCORING GUIDE OR RUBRIC

A rubric is simply a guide for evaluating performance, and is presented below.

FIGURE 4.1 WAITER/WAITRESS RUBRIC

	Level One	Level Two	Level Three	Level Four
Courtesy				
Appearance				
Responsiveness				
Knowledge				
Coordination				
Accuracy				

In the left column are listed the different criteria we have determined are important for waiters and waitresses in our fledgling restaurant. Across the top are four columns for different levels of performance. In this case, there are four levels, and the double line between levels two and three indicates that performance at levels three and four is acceptable, and performance at levels one and two is unacceptable. We could, then, broadly define the different levels as:

Level One: "Very poor," or "Terrible" or "Completely unacceptable"
Level Two: "Not quite good enough," or "Almost"
Level Three: "Acceptable," or "Good enough but not great"
Level Four: "Wonderful," "Exemplary," or "Terrific"

In each box, then, we would write descriptions of actual performance that would represent each level for each criterion. For example, for "coordination" we might decide that an individual at level one actually spilled an entire bowl of soup, or a cup of coffee, or could not handle a tray of dishes; someone at level two spilled a little coffee in the saucer, or let some water spill while filling the glasses; a waiter at level three spilled nothing, and someone at level four balanced many items without mishap.

We could fill in the entire chart with such descriptions, and we would then be ready to go evaluate prospective employees. A possible profile might look like the following:

FIGURE 4.2 COMPLETED WAITER/WAITRESS RUBRIC

Name   Wendy Jones   Restaurant   Hilltop Cafe

	Level One	Level Two	Level Three	Level Four
Courtesy		X		
Appearance				X
Responsiveness			X	
Knowledge	X			
Coordination				X
Accuracy			X	

We would still have to decide, of course, whether to hire this individual. Or whether this individual was preferable to another candidate whose scores were all '3's.' That is, we would have to determine how to arrive at a composite score for each individual, so we could compare them.

Naturally, if we were using this approach not for hiring, but for supervision, we would not need to combine scores on the different criteria; we could use them simply for feedback and coaching. For example, since this individual is, apparently, not very knowledgeable, we could provide assistance in that area. We could then work on courtesy, and make sure that customers feel comfortable around this person. That is, for supervision purposes, the system is diagnostic, and enables us, as owners of the restaurant, to provide specific and substantive feedback on areas needing improvement.

SUMMARY

Creating a scoring rubric for a non-school activity provides an illustration of the principles involved in performance assessment.

MEASUREMENT AND PRACTICAL ISSUES

When we contemplate applying these principles to the evaluation of student performance, we encounter a number of issues which, while not technically complex, must be addressed before this approach can be implemented. It should be borne in mind, however, that most teachers have rubrics in their minds for student performance; they apply these every time they grade a student's paper. However, communication is vastly improved if educators can be explicit about the criteria they use in evaluating student work, and what their expectations are. This need for clarity requires us to address a number of technical and practical issues, which are described below.

THE NUMBER AND TYPE OF CRITERIA

For a given performance, how many criteria should we have? For example, when evaluating a persuasive essay, how many different things should we look for? Should we evaluate organization separately from structure? What about the use of language? Or specifically, the use of vocabulary? Or correct spelling and mechanics? What about sentence structure and organization? Should we consider the essay's impact on us, the reader? Is it important that we are actually persuaded by the argument?

Clearly, some of these elements are related to one another; it would be difficult, in a persuasive essay, to have good use of language independently of the vocabulary used. However, other criteria are completely separate from one another. Unless it is so poor as to hinder communication, a student's inadequacies in mechanics and spelling will not affect the persuasiveness of the argument.

The number of criteria used should reflect, insofar as it is possible to predict, those aspects of performance which are simultaneously important and are independent of one another. They will also reflect the age and skill of the students. For example, with young children or special education students it might be necessary to identify specific aspects of punctuation that are evaluated, i.e., proper use of capital letters, commas, and semi-colons, whereas for high school students these may all be clustered under "punctuation" and can include all aspects of mechanics.

However, when criteria are clustered in such a way that they include several elements, these should be specifically identified. Just as, in the waiter and waitress example, "appearance" might include the person's uniform, condition of the hair and nails, and general grooming, individual criteria should specify what elements are included. For example, "use of language" might include richness of vocabulary, use of persuasive words, and proper use of specialized terms.

The criteria, moreover, should reflect those aspects of performance which are truly most important, not merely those which are easiest to see or count. Thus, a rubric for writing should include more than spelling and mechanics; a rubric for problem-solving should include criteria dealing with the student's thought processes and methods of approach.

A rubric should not include so many criteria that it is difficult to use. On the other hand, it should include every important element. As a general rule, since most people cannot hold more than five or six items in their mind simultaneously, rubrics should not contain more than five or six criteria.

ANALYTIC VS. HOLISTIC RUBRICS

The waiter/waitress rubric developed in the previous section is an example of an *analytic* rubric, that is, different criteria are identified and levels of performance are described for each. Using such a rubric in the classroom, in which different criteria are defined and described, makes it possible to analyze student work as to its strengths and weaknesses.

With a *holistic* rubric, on the other hand, the features of performance on all criteria for a given score are combined, so it is possible, for example, to describe a "level two" waiter, or a "level four" waitress. Such holistic judgments are necessary when a single score, such as on an Advanced Placement test, must be given. However, compromises are always necessary, since an individual piece of work will usually not include all the features of a certain level. Therefore, analytic rubrics are recommended for classroom use, since they provide much more complete information to be used for feedback to students.

However, even for classroom use, when rubrics are used to evaluate student work, they may be applied either analytically or holistically. That is, student performance may be evaluated on each element of the rubric, and feedback provided on each. Alternatively, a teacher can examine a piece of student work as a whole, and apply a rubric more holistically. Which approach is used will depend on the amount, and level of detail, of feedback desired. For the samples of student work included in this book, the rubrics are written analytically, but they are applied holistically. This permits careful analysis of each student work sample, yet an efficient summary of the salient features of each.

HOW MANY POINTS ON THE SCALE?

In the waiter/waitress example, we identified four points

on the scale. That was an arbitrary decision; we could have selected more, or fewer. Performance on any criterion, after all, falls along a continuum; designating points on a scale represents, to some degree, a compromise between practical demands and the complexity of real performance. However, in deciding on the number of points to use, there are two important considerations to bear in mind:

- *Fineness of distinctions.* More points offer the opportunity to make very fine distinctions between levels of performance. However, scales with many points are time-consuming to use, since the differences between different points are likely to be small.

- *Even vs. odd.* In general an even number of points is preferable to an odd number. This relates to the measurement principle of "central tendency," which states that many people, if given the opportunity, will assign a score in the middle of a range. If there is no middle, as on a scale with an even number of points, they are required to make a commitment to one side or the other.

However, these considerations apply to rubrics that are constructed to apply to a single activity or type of performance. For developmental rubrics, a large number of points may be preferable. In a developmental rubric, students' performance over an extended period of time is monitored on a single rubric. Used most commonly in Foreign Language classes, such a rubric might define oral language proficiency from the most rudimentary through the level displayed by a native speaker. Every student of the language will perform somewhere, at all times, on that rubric, which might have, perhaps 10 points. A second-year student might be functioning at, say, level "3," while a fourth-year student might be at level "5." Both would have made good progress, and yet would have a distance to go before performing at the level of a native speaker. For such purposes, a developmental rubric with many points on the scale is extremely useful, since it can be used to chart progress over many years.

DIVIDING LINE BETWEEN ACCEPTABLE AND UNACCEPTABLE PERFORMANCE

It is important to decide at the outset where the line will be between acceptable and unacceptable performance. This activity is at the heart of setting a standard, since teachers thereby communicate to their colleagues as well as their students, the quality of work they expect.

In the waiter/waitress example, the line between acceptable and unacceptable performance was established between levels "2" and "3." This, too, is arbitrary; it could just as well been put between the "1" and the "2." When determining where to place the dividing line, educators should consider several points:

- *Use.* If a scoring rubric is to be used for formative evaluation, it is helpful to identify several levels of "unacceptable," since, in that way, teachers can know quickly whether a student's performance on a certain criterion is close to being acceptable or far away. Such knowledge can guide further instruction. On the other hand, if a rubric is to be used to make a summative judgment only, then it is less important if a student's performance is close to the cut-off point; in this case, unacceptable is unacceptable, without regard to degrees of unacceptability.

- *Number of points on the scale.* If a scoring rubric is constructed with six, seven, or eight points, then the placement of the "unacceptable" line might be different from a rubric with only four points. A five-point scale (while not ideal from the standpoint of having an odd number of points) enables two levels of unacceptable while also permitting finer degrees of excellence, with the upper levels representing "barely acceptable," "good," and "excellent."

- *Developmental vs. performance-specific rubrics.* Clearly, for a developmental rubric, one that defines performance over an extended period of time, there is no need to define the distinction between "acceptable" and "unacceptable" performance in the same manner as for a performance-specific rubric. That is, it may be reasonable for a second-year language student to perform at level "3" on a ten-point scale, whereas such performance would not be good enough for a fourth-year student. In this case, judgments as to acceptability and expectations do not reside in the rubric, but in the use that is made of them in different settings.

TITLES FOR LEVELS OF PERFORMANCE

Closely related to the need to define the cut-off between acceptable and unacceptable performance is the requirement to broadly define the labels for each point on the rubric. For professional use, teachers often use terms like "unacceptable," and "exemplary." Such titles might work even if students (or their parents) will see the rubric, but it should be given some thought. Some educators prefer names like "novice," "emerging," "proficient," and "distinguished." Decisions as to the best headings are matters for professional judgment and consensus.

DESCRIPTIONS OF PERFORMANCE

Descriptions for levels of performance should be written in language that is truly descriptive, rather than comparative. For example, words such as "average" should be avoided, as in "the number of computational errors is average," and replaced by statements such as "the solution contains only minor computational errors." "Minor" will then have to be defined, for example, as an error not resulting in an erroneous conclusion, or an error that was clearly based in carelessness.

GENERIC VS. TASK-SPECIFIC

Constructing a performance rubric for student work takes considerable time, particularly if it is a joint effort among many educators. The issue of time, combined with the desirability of sending a consistent signal to students and their parents regarding standards, are important reasons to try to create generic rubrics. Such rubrics may be used for many different specific tasks that students do.

The areas of student performance that appear to lend themselves best to generic rubrics are such things as lab reports, problem-solving, expository (descriptive or persuasive) essays, group projects, and oral presentations. Some of these, such as oral presentations, may even be suitable for several different disciplines. It is highly valuable for students to know that when they are preparing an oral presentation, it will always be evaluated, in every course, using the same criteria.

Generic rubrics however, are not always possible or even desirable. The elements of problem-solving, and certainly the levels of acceptable performance are very different for high school sophomores than those for second graders. Similarly, the specific elements of a lab report change as students become more sophisticated and more knowledgeable. So while there are many reasons to construct rubrics as generic as possible — and intra- and cross-departmental discussions are highly recommended — it may not be possible to completely develop generic rubrics, even for those aspects of performance in which students are engaged over a period of many years. There are many tasks, and many types of tasks, which require their own task-specific rubrics.

PROFESSIONAL CONSENSUS

When teachers work together to determine descriptions of levels of performance in a scoring rubric, they may find that they do not completely agree. This is natural and to be expected. After all, it is well documented that teachers grade student work quite differently from one another.

Discussions as to the proper wording of different levels of performance constitute rich professional dialogue. While difficult, the discussions are generally enriching for everyone involved; most teachers find that their ideas can be enhanced by the contributions of their colleagues. Rubrics that are the product of many minds are generally superior to those created by individuals. In addition, if a number of teachers find that they can use the same, or similar, rubrics for evaluating student work, communication with students is that much more consistent, resulting in better quality work.

INTER-RATER AGREEMENT

Closely related to consensus on the wording of descriptions of levels of performance is the matter of agreement on the application of the rubric. The only way to be sure that different individuals agree on the meaning of the descriptions of different levels is to actually apply the statements to samples of student work.

The importance of this issue cannot be exaggerated. It is a fundamental principle of equity and fairness that evaluation of a student's work be the same regardless of who is doing the evaluating. However, teachers very rarely agree completely at the beginning. Occasionally, two teachers will evaluate a single piece of student work very differently, even when they have agreed on the scoring rubric. In those cases, they generally discover that they were interpreting words in the rubric very differently, or that the words used were themselves ambiguous. Only trying the rubric with actual student work will reveal such difficulties.

When preparing rubrics for evaluating student work, therefore, the project is not totally complete until examples of different levels of performance have been selected to illustrate the points on the scale. Called "anchor papers" these samples can serve to maintain consistency in scoring.

CLARITY OF DIRECTIONS

Another fundamental principle of fairness and equity concerns the directions given to students. Any criterion to be evaluated must be clearly asked for in the directions to a performance task. For example, if students are to be evaluated for their originality in making an oral presentation, something in the directions to them should recommend that they present it in an original or creative manner. Likewise, if students are to be evaluated for the organization of their data, they should know that organization is important. Otherwise, from a student's point of view, it is necessary to read the mind of the teacher and to guess what is important.

Some teachers find that they can engage students in the development of the rubric itself. Students, they discover, know the indicators of a good oral presentation or of a well-solved problem. While students' thoughts are rarely well enough organized to enable them to create a rubric on their own, their ideas make good additions to a rubric already drafted by the teacher.

There are many advantages to engaging students in the construction of a scoring rubric. Most obviously, they know what is included and can therefore focus their work. But even more important, students tend to do better work, with greater pride in it and greater attention to quality when the evaluation criteria are clear. Suddenly, school is not a matter of "gotcha," it is a place where excellent work is both defined and expected.

COMBINING SCORES ON CRITERIA

Occasionally, it is important to be able to combine scores on different criteria and to arrive at a single evaluation. For example, teachers must occasionally rank students, or convert their judgments on performance to a grade or to a percentage. How can this be done? In arriving at a single, holistic score, several issues must be addressed:

- *Weight.* Are all the criteria of equal importance? Unless one or another is designated as more or less important than the others, they should all be assumed to be of equal importance. Educators should have good reasons for their decisions as to weight, and these discussions can themselves constitute important professional conversations. As an example, we could have determined, in our creation of the rubric for a waiter or waitress, that "knowledge" is the most important criterion and is worth twice the value of the others. Then, our rubric and the points possible from each point, appear on the following page:

- *Calculations.* How should the scores be calculated?

FIGURE 4.3 WAITER/WAITRESS RUBRIC

Name ___Wendy Jones___   Restaurant ___Hilltop Cafe___

	Level One	Level Two	Level Three	Level Four
Courtesy Weight = 1		X		
Appearance Weight = 1				X
Responsiveness Weight = 1			X	
Knowledge Weight = 2	X			
Coordination Weight = 1				X
Accuracy Weight = 1			X	

Scores: (score assigned) x (weight) = (criterion score)
  criterion score on each criterion = total score
  total score / total possible scores = percentage score

Using this procedure for Wendy Jones, her point score would be as follows:

Courtesy:	2 (2 x 1)
Appearance:	4 (4 x 1)
Responsiveness:	3 (3 x 1)
Knowledge:	2 (1 x 2)
Coordination:	4 (4 x 1)
Accuracy:	3 (3 x 1)
Total:	18

On this rubric, the total possible points for each criterion are:

Courtesy: 4
Appearance: 4
Responsiveness: 4
Knowledge: 8
Responsiveness: 4
Accuracy: 4

Total points: 28

Therefore, to calculate a total score, we convert the points received to a percentage of the total possible points. Both the points received and the number of possible points reflect the weights assigned to each criterion. Thus, in our example of Wendy Jones, she would have received a score of 18, which, when divided by 28 is 64%.

- *Cut score.* What is the overall level of acceptable performance? We have, of course, defined the line between acceptable and unacceptable performance for each criterion earlier. However, now we must determine a score which, overall, represents acceptable performance. We could set it as a percentage, for example 70%, in which case Wendy Jones would not be hired in our restaurant. Alternatively, we could establish a rule that no more than one criterion may be rated at a score below "3." This decision, like all the others made in constructing a performance rubric, is a matter of professional judgment.

TIME

Both for large-scale assessment and in the classroom, teachers know that multiple choice, short-answer, matching, and true/false tests take far less time to score than essay or open-ended tests. It is a relatively simple matter to take a stack of student tests and grade them against an answer key. Many educators fear that using performance tasks and rubrics will consume more time than they have or want to devote to it.

There is some validity to this concern. It is true that the evaluation of student work, using a rubric, takes more time than does grading student tests against a key. Also, the rubric itself can take considerable time to create.

However, there are two important issues to consider, one related to the increasing ease of using performance tasks, and the second related to the benefits derived from their use.

* *Decreasing time demands.* When they are just beginning to use performance tasks and rubrics, many teachers find that the time requirements are far greater than those needed for traditional tests. However, as they become more skilled, and as the rubrics they have developed prove to be useful for other assignments or other types of work, they discover that they can evaluate student work very efficiently, and in many cases in less time than the time required for traditional tests.

* *Other benefits.* In any event, most teachers discover that the benefits derived from increased use of performance tasks and rubrics vastly outweigh the additional time needed. They discover that students produce better quality work, and that they take greater pride in that work. If used as a component in assigning grades, teachers find that they can justify their decisions far more reliably than before they were using rubrics.

"SUBJECTIVITY" VS. "OBJECTIVITY"

One of the most important reservations about the use of rubrics to evaluate student work concerns their perceived "subjectivity" compared to "objective" multiple-choice tests. Such fears, while understandable, are completely unjustified.

First, it is important to remember that the only objective feature to a multiple-choice test is its scoring; answers are unambiguously right or wrong. However, many professional judgments have entered into making the test, and even into determining which of the possible answers are the correct ones. Someone must decide what questions to ask and how to structure the problems. These decisions reflect a vision of what is important knowledge and skill for students to demonstrate, and are based on professional judgment.

Similarly, in the construction of a scoring rubric, many decisions must be made; these, too, are made on the basis of professional judgment. But the fact that they are made by teachers in their classrooms, rather than by testing companies, does not make them less valid judgmentally. In fact, it may be argued that, if well thought out, such judgements are superior to those made by anonymous agencies far from the realities of one's own classrom.

In any event, scoring rubrics to evaluate student work, and standardized tests are both grounded in professional judgment; they are absolutely equivalent on that score. In both cases, it is the quality of the judgments that is important, and the classroom-based judgment may be as good as that made by the testing company.

SUMMARY

In using scoring rubrics to evaluate student work, many issues must be taken into consideration. However, these issues, such as the number of points on the scale, or the importance of inter-rater agreement, are primarily a matter of common sense.

5

CREATING A PERFORMANCE TASK

The evaluation plan which results from the analysis of curriculum outcomes and topics (determined in Chapter 3) provides the guidelines needed to actually design performance tasks. As part of that plan, educators will have decided which topics or units lend themselves to the corresponding outcome goals or strands, and will have determined the best evaluation strategy for each. This analysis provides the basis for developing specifications (or requirements) for each performance task.

It is important to remember that a performance task is not simply something fun to do with one's students; it is not merely an activity. While it may involve student activity, and it may be fun, it is highly purposeful. A performance task is designed to assess learning, and it must be designed with that fundamental purpose in mind. In the design of performance tasks, a number of factors must be taken into consideration. These are described in this chapter.

SIZE OF PERFORMANCE TASKS

Performance tasks may be large or small. Large tasks take on many of the characteristics of instructional units, and students tend to derive much benefit from them. Large tasks may require a week or more to complete. They are typically complex and authentic, and require students to synthesize information from many sources. Small tasks, on the other hand, are more like open-ended test questions in which students solve a problem and explain their reasoning. These may be completed in a single class period or less. Naturally, tasks may be of medium length and complexity.

In deciding whether to use performance tasks that are large or small, educators must take a number of factors into account. These are outlined below.

PURPOSE

Teachers should be very clear about their purpose in using the performance task. What do they hope and plan to derive from it? Are their purposes purely those of assessment, or do they hope to accomplish some instructional purposes as well?

* *Small tasks are primarily suitable for purely assessment purposes.* If a teacher has taught a concept, for example the distinction between area and perimeter, and simply wants to know that students have understood that concept, then a small performance task is desirable. Such a task will ask students to solve a relatively small problem, to explain their thinking, and to show their work. However, it will not, in itself, also contain activities to be completed as part of the task. The task itself is designed purely for assessment.

* *Large tasks carry instructional purposes as well as assessment ones.* Occasionally, a teacher will want students to truly learn new content as a result of completing an assessment task. If so, a larger task, spread over a number of days, involving many sub-activities, will accomplish this purpose better than a small task.

* *Large tasks are better suited to culminating assessments than are small ones.* If performance tasks are to be used as culminating assessments, they are better if they are quite large and tap a number of different types of skills. However, if performance tasks are for the purpose of assessing a small part of the curriculum, small tasks are more useful since they can be administered frequently and the results used for

adjusting instruction. The purpose of the assessment will be a major factor, then, in determining whether performance tasks should be large or small.

CURRICULUM PRESSURE AND TIME DEMANDS

Generally speaking, when teachers are under pressure to "cover" many topics in the curriculum, and consequently have little time to spend on any one topic, they may find that small performance tasks are all that they have time for. Large tasks, while they include many benefits not derived from small ones, do require lots of time, frequently more than many teachers have to devote to them.

SKILL IN GETTING STARTED

Most educators, when they are just beginning to use performance tasks, are unsure of what they are doing; in such situations it is a good idea to use the "start small" principle. For example, when not sure whether the directions to students on a task are clear, it is better to discover that after the students have spent a class period, rather than a week, completing the task. Less time has been lost and there may well be an opportunity to attempt another version of the same task, or a different task, later.

SUMMARY

The size of a performance task is best determined by its purpose (immediate or culminating assessment, or instruction) and by the time constraints and experience of the teacher. In general, it is recommended that teachers begin their efforts with performance assessment using tasks which are small rather than large. This provides the opportunity to experiment with a new methodology in a way that carries low stakes for success, for both the students and the teacher.

CRITERIA FOR GOOD PERFORMANCE TASKS

There is no doubt that some performance tasks are better

than others. What makes the good ones good? How can teachers, in designing or selecting performance tasks ensure that they are as good as possible? Several important qualities of good performance tasks are described below.

ENGAGING

The most important single criterion of performance tasks is that they are engaging to students; it is essential that they be of interest and that students want to put forth their best effort. This suggests that the questions asked have intrinsic merit so that students don't read the question and respond "So what?" or "Who cares?"

How does one find or create engaging tasks? As with so much else in education, professional judgment is the key. Successful instructional activities can be a good place to begin; most teachers know which activities, or which types of activities, are successful with their students. One of these activities, when adapted to the demands of assessment, might make a good performance task. And when reviewing tasks that others have created, one important criterion to always bear in mind is whether the task is likely to be engaging to students.

AUTHENTICITY

Related to engagement is the issue of authenticity. Students tend to be more interested in those situations that resemble "real life" rather than those which are completely divorced from any practical application. In addition, performance tasks that reflect the "messiness" of real life make demands on students that more sanitized situations do not. Other things being equal, it is preferable to design or adapt performance tasks that represent authentic applications of knowledge and skill. Such authenticity requires students to use their knowledge and skill in much the same way it is used by adult practitioners in that field. A "template" to be used for designing authentic tasks is provided as Figure 5.2 at the end of the chapter.

However, authenticity is not always possible. Some important school learning is purely abstract, or makes sense only within its own context. For example, when we want students to demonstrate that they can analyze a character in literature, we must ask them to do that, even though such a task has no exact equivalents in "real life." Furthermore, a student's skill in analyzing a literary character assesses not only how well the student understands the character, but the degree to which he or she understands the structure of the piece of literature of which the character is a part.

Similarly, much of mathematics is highly formal and abstract. And while teachers care that students can apply their mathematical knowledge to practical situations, there is much of mathematics, such as number theory, which is internal to the discipline. But such knowledge must be assessed, and a constructed-response question is preferable to a multiple-choice item. However, such a question will probably not reflect authentic application.

ELICITS DESIRED KNOWLEDGE AND SKILL

A good performance task must assess what we want it to assess. It must, in other words, be aligned to the instructional goals we are interested in. Furthermore, the task should be designed in such a way that a student can complete the task correctly only by using the knowledge and skills being assessed.

We should never underestimate our students in this regard. While most students are not devious, most try to complete a task with as little risk and/or effort as possible. If they see an easy way to do the task, even by short-circuiting our intentions, they may well do it that way. Teachers should attempt, therefore, to create tasks that are as tight as possible, without being unduly rigid.

ENABLES ASSESSMENT OF INDIVIDUALS

Many performance tasks that sound imaginative are designed to be completed by students working in groups. And while such tasks may be valuable instructional activities and are certainly fun for the students, they cannot be used for the assessment of individuals. Assessment, after all, concerns the evaluation of individual learning; a performance task in which the contributions of different individuals is obscured cannot be used for such evaluation.

It is possible, of course, to design a performance task that includes both group and individual elements. For example, a group of students may be given some data and asked to analyze it. However, if the analysis is done as a group, each student should be required to produce an independent summary of what the data shows, and each individual's paper should be evaluated independently.

However, even in such a situation, the information for the teacher is somewhat compromised. When reading the work of an individual, a teacher knows only what that student could produce after having participated in a group with other students. With a different group of peers, that same student might have demonstrated much greater, or far less, understanding.

In general, then, it is preferable to create individual performance tasks if these are to be used solely for assessment purposes. If the goal also includes instructional purposes, then compromises on the individuality of the assessment tasks may be necessary.

CONTAINS CLEAR DIRECTIONS FOR STUDENTS

Any good performance task includes directions for students that are both complete and unambiguous. This is a fundamental principle of equity and good measurement. Students should never be in doubt about what it is they are to do on a performance task; the directions should be clear and complete. That does not mean that the directions should be lengthy; on the contrary, shorter directions are preferable to longer ones.

Secondly, the directions should specifically ask students to do everything on which they will be evaluated. For example, if one of the assessment criteria for a mathematics problem involves the organization of information, students should be specifically instructed to "present their information in an organized manner," or some such wording.

Related to the question of directions is that of scaffolding, that is, how much support should students receive in accomplishing the performance task? For example, in a mathematics problem that involves a multi-step solution, should the students be prompted for each step, or is that part of the problem? The answer to this question relates to the purposes of the assessment, and the age and skill level of the students. Less scaffolding is more authentic than more scaffolding; most problems are not presented to us with an outline of how to solve them. In general it is preferable to provide students with problems, with no scaffolding, that represent the optimal challenge for them to determine the proper approach on their own. An intermediate position is to present the problem, with no scaffolding, and then offer "tips" to the student to consider if desired. These tips can contain suggestions that, if followed, would provide guidance as to a possible approach to the problem.

SUMMARY

Good performance tasks share a number of important criteria. These should be borne in mind as tasks are designed.

THE DESIGN PROCESS

Now that the criteria for a performance task are clearly in mind, it is time to create one. What process should be followed? While there are several possible approaches, an effective one is described below.

CREATE AN INITIAL DESIGN

With the specifications and criteria in mind, create an initial draft of a performance task to assess a given combination of student understanding and skill. This task may be created using the format provided as Figure 5.1 at the end of the chapter, and it may, if authenticity is desired, follow the "template" offered in Figure 5.2. This initial draft should be considered as just that, an initial draft; it will almost certainly be revised later in the process.

OBTAIN COLLEAGUE REVIEW

If possible, persuade one or more colleagues to review your work. These may be teachers who work in the same discipline as you or with the same age students, or they may be teachers with very different responsibilities. Both approaches have their advantages and their drawbacks.

Teachers with different responsibilities are more likely to catch ambiguity or lack of clarity in the directions to students than are teachers who are as expert in the field as you are. On the other hand, expert colleagues are better able to spot situations in which the task is not completely valid, that is, situations in which students would be able to complete the task successfully without the desired knowledge and skill. Therefore, a colleague review that includes a combination of content experts and non-experts is ideal.

PILOT TASK WITH STUDENTS

Not until a performance task is tried with students is it possible to know whether it can accomplish its desired purpose. Only then can teachers know whether the directions are clear, whether all elements are properly requested, and whether the task truly elicits the desired knowledge and skill. Piloting with students is also the only way to know the degree to which the task is engaging to students.

Students are likely to be extremely honest in their reaction to a performance task. While it is possible to collect their feedback formally, it is generally evident, from their level of engagement and the quality of their responses, whether the task is a good one or not.

REVISE PERFORMANCE TASK

As a result of the colleague review and the pilot with students, the draft task will, no doubt, require some revision. This revision might be a major rewrite. More likely, it will be a minor revision in order to make the task clearer, less cumbersome, or differently slanted.

Once revised, the task is ready for the formal process of rubric design discussed in Chapter 6. However, teachers should be aware that the task may need further revision after the scoring rubric is written; that exercise frequently reveals inadequacies (usually minor) in the task itself.

SUMMARY

The process of task design has several steps, all of which should be completed. A performance task should not be used for actual assessment until it has been piloted with students. This suggests that at least a year will elapse between the decision to embark on a program of performance assessment and the implementation of such a system.

FIGURE 5.1 PERFORMANCE TASK DESIGN WORKSHEET

Course _____ Topic _____

Outcome(s) _____

_____

Task Title

Brief description of the task (what students must do, and what product will result

Directions to the students:

Criteria to be used to evaluate student responses

FIGURE 5.2 PERFORMANCE TASK. AUTHENTIC SIMULATION

Outcome: _____

Topic: _____

You are (student or adult role or profession)

Who has been asked by (audience or superior)

To (accomplish a specific task)

Using (resources)

Under the constraints of (as found in such a situation)

Your work will be judged according to (criteria)

(Attach a rubric)

Based on Worksheets from the High Success Network and CLASS

6

CREATING A RUBRIC

In order to use a performance task to evaluate student learning, a guide for evaluating student work, such as a rubric, is needed. The development of the task and the application of the rubric should be considered an iterative process (as each is developed and used it suggests changes in the other) with the final combination of task and rubric evolving over time. This section includes guidance for the design of a rubric for a task.

DRAFTING A SCORING RUBRIC

Generally speaking, the criteria to be used in evaluating student work will have been identified in the course of developing a performance task. However, in order to convert these criteria into an actual scoring rubric, they must be elaborated and further defined. While holistic rubrics have their uses (e.g., in the summative evaluation of student work for awarding a diploma), this section will focus on the design of analytic rubrics. A general format for developing a rubric is provided in Figure 6.1.

GENERIC OR TASK-SPECIFIC?

The first question to be answered concerns the degree of task-specificity of the rubric. If, for example, the rubric is being developed for a group mathematics project, could the same rubric be used for other projects, or is its use confined to this particular one? Indeed, could the elements of the rubric,

FIGURE 6.1 PERFORMANCE RUBRIC

Criteria	(Activity)			
	1	2	3	4

concerned with making a group presentation, be used for other disciplines as well? Are there enough similarities between group presentations for mathematics, science, and social studies that the same evaluation guide could be used for all of them?

In general, of course, generic rubrics are more useful that task-specific ones. Creating rubrics is time-consuming and the more broadly they may be applied, the more useful and powerful they are. However, sometimes a common rubric will have to be adapted for use in other situations and in other disciplines; while many of the elements are the same, the ways in which they appear in student work are sufficiently different to warrant independent consideration.

TASK OR GENRE SPECIFIC, OR DEVELOPMENTAL

Another important question to be considered when creating a rubric is whether the rubric will be used on a single task (or a single type of task) or whether it will be used developmentally with students as they progress through many years of school. That is, will the rubric under development for a mathematics project, be applied for only this particular project which students do in the seventh grade, or could it be used also with students throughout the district, including those in elementary school as well as in high school?

If the rubric is to be used developmentally, it will probably have many more points on it, and the criteria may be written differently than if the rubric is to be used for a single task. A developmental rubric is useful for a school in which students have mathematics portfolios, and may be helpful in charting progress over time. However, a developmental rubric may not be as useful for any particular task as one created specifically for that task.

DETERMINING CRITERIA

Once the question of task-specificity or developmental rubric has been answered, the most important single step in creating a scoring rubric is to identify the criteria to be evaluated. The importance of attending carefully to this step cannot be overstated. It is in the determination of criteria that educators define important aspects of performance, and define, both for themselves and their students, what they mean by good quality. When defining criteria, several issues should be considered.

- *Type of criteria.* In mathematics, an essential criterion almost always concerns mathematical accuracy. Is the answer correct? Are computational errors major or minor? Are answers correctly labeled? Are all possible answers found?

  But in addition to computational accuracy, what else is important? What about conceptual understanding? Do students reveal, either through their approach to the problem or through the errors they make, that they have no understanding of the underlying concepts? Does the problem require a plan? If so, have students organized their information? Have they approached the problem in a systematic manner? Is the work presented neatly? Can a reader follow the student's line of reasoning?

In addition, a mathematics project might require that students collaborate together. How successfully do they do this? Do they establish a good division of labor, or do one or two students dominate the group? If the students make a presentation as part of the project, do they explain their thinking clearly? Are the other students interested in the presentation? Can they follow it? Is it engaging? It is important that the criteria identified for a task not consist only of those that are easiest to see, such as computational accuracy. The criteria should, taken together, define all the aspects of exemplary performance, even if some of them are somewhat challenging to specify and to evaluate.

One successful approach to the identification of criteria is to consider the task and to imagine an excellent student response to it. What would such a response include? The answer to that question can serve to identify important criteria. Alternatively, many teachers do the task themselves prior to assigning it to their students, creating in effect, an exemplary response, and appreciating the issues inherent in the task for students.

- *Number and detail of criteria.* There is no single best answer to the question of "how many criteria?" Clearly, all important aspects of performance should be captured in the criteria. Moreover, those aspects of performance that are independent of one another should be designated as separate criteria.

It is possible to designate too many criteria, and for them to be too detailed. The resulting rubric is then cumbersome and time-consuming to use. On the other hand, a rubric that is too economical may not provide adequate information to students for them to improve performance. The number and level of detail of the rubric then, is partly a matter of how it is to be used and the age and skill level of the students. Rubrics used with special needs students, for example, are often made in great detail, so both teachers and students are aware of where improvement efforts should be focused.

- *Sub-criteria or elements.* Sometimes, several criteria are related to one another or one may be considered a sub-category of another. In that case, the criteria may contain within them sub-criteria or elements. For example, if students make a presentation as part of the mathematics project, the overall criterion might be "quality of presentation" with sub-criteria of "clarity," "originality and energy," and "involvement of all group members."

Occasionally, when educators think critically about the qualities they would look for in good student performance, they recognize that the task, as written, does not elicit those qualities; they then return to the task and alter the student directions. That is, students could do the task and not demonstrate the criteria that have been defined. In that case, the directions must be rewritten, or the task restructured, to elicit the desired performance.

NUMBER OF POINTS

The question of the number of points on a scoring scale is closely related, of course, to whether the rubric is task-specific or developmental. If developmental, it will almost certainly have more points than if it is task-specific and the number of points should reflect the age range over which the rubric will be applied. For a skill, such as problem-solving or graphing that develops from kindergarten through 12th grade, a scale with 10 points would be reasonable.

But even for task-specific rubrics, educators must decide on the number of points. As explained previously, an even number is preferable to an odd number, since it prevents the phenomenon known as "central tendency." But beyond that, there are several considerations to keep in mind.

- *Detail in distinctions.* With a larger number of points on a scale, fine distinctions are required when evaluating student work. While such detail can provide finely-tuned feedback to students, a rubric with many points is cumbersome and time-consuming to use. For practical purposes, a rubric with 4-6 points is recommended. The ones in this collection all contain four points.

- *Dividing line between acceptable and unacceptable performance.* It is helpful, at the outset, to determine the dividing line between acceptable and unacceptable performance. On a four-point scale, this line is either between the "1" and the "2" or between the "2" and the "3." That placement will be determined by where the greater detail is the more useful; that is, is it more useful to be able to specify degrees of inadequacy or degrees of adequacy?

- *General headings for different points.* The different points on the scale may be called simply by their numbers. On a four-point scale then, they would be 0, 1, 2, and 3 or 1, 2, 3, and 4. Alternatively, they could be 10, 20, 30, and 40. Alternatively, the points can be given names such as "novice," "proficient," "exemplary," "great!" If this approach is taken, it is preferable to use positive, supportive words (such as "emerging") rather than negative ones (such as "inadequate").

DESCRIPTIONS OF LEVELS OF PERFORMANCE

Once the criteria and the number of scale points have been determined, it is time to actually write the descriptions of performance levels. Again, this step is critical and includes a number of factors.

- *The language used.* The words used to specify the qualities of different levels of performance should be descriptive, rather than comparative. For example, words such as "average" should be avoided. The descriptions of performance levels serve to further define the criteria, and are further defined themselves only when accompanied by actual samples of student work, called anchor papers.

- *All sub-criteria or elements defined.* If the criteria contain sub-criteria within them, each of these elements should be described in each of the performance descriptions. For example, if a criterion on presentation includes accuracy and originality, and involvement of all group members, then the descriptions for each of the levels should describe the group's presentation with respect to all those elements.

- *Distance between points.* To the extent possible, the distance between the points on a scale should be equal. That is, the distance between a "3" and a "4" should not be much greater than that between a "2" and a "3."

- *The line between acceptable and unacceptable performance.* Placement of the line between acceptable and unacceptable performance should receive particular scrutiny. While the highest and lowest levels of performance are the easiest to describe, those in the middle, that define acceptable and unacceptable performance, are the most important. It is here, after all, that educators define their standards and specify the quality of work on which they insist and expect mastery. It is recommended that this level be described with particular care.

SUMMARY

The most critical step in the development of a scoring rubric for evaluating student performance is its initial design. For this process, a number of factors — such as whether it is generic or specific, the actual criteria, the number of points on the scale, and the language used to define the points — must be taken into account.

PILOTING THE RUBRIC WITH STUDENT WORK

The proof of a rubric is in its use with student work, and not until a rubric is used to evaluate actual student work will its authors know whether it is viable. Several steps are recommended.

EVALUATING A SAMPLE OF STUDENT WORK

A good place to begin is to collect a small number of samples (about 8) of students' work, representing the full range of probable responses in the class. The sample should include those students from whom the best work would be expected, as well as those whose work might not be adequate. If possible, the pieces of work should be anonymous; they could be numbered and referred to by their numbers.

Then, with the rubric in hand, evaluate the student work using the draft rubric. The form shown in Fig. 6.2 may be used, with the criteria listed (or numbered) down the side, and the levels of performance for different students specified in the column corresponding to each one. Surveying the entire page then, provides a summary of the levels of performance represented by the class as a whole, and can offer guidance as to the next instructional steps that may be needed.

FIGURE 6.2 PERFORMANCE ASSESSMENT EVALUATION RESULTS

Evaluator _____ Date _____

Task _____ Grade Level _____

Student Criteria	Student 1	Student 2	Student 3	Student 4	Student 5	Student 6	Student 7	Student 8

INTER-RATER AGREEMENT

Even with careful design, it is possible that the rubric or the use of the rubric, is not yet reliable. The only way to check this is to request assistance from a colleague. It is recommended that another educator be introduced to the task and the rubric, and be provided with the same sample of student work initially used. This person should then evaluate the same students, and assign scores on each criterion based on the draft rubric.

Scores for each student on each criterion should then be compared. Clearly, the goal is for all scores to be the same, although this is unlikely to occur. Any discrepancies should then be discussed until the cause of the discrepancy is understood; most frequently, discrepancies are caused by a lack of clarity in the words used in the performance levels.

REVISING THE RUBRIC (AND POSSIBLY ALSO THE TASK)

As a result of evaluating student work and of comparing scores assigned with those of another educator, it is likely that the rubric (and possibly also the task) will require some revision. With luck, these revisions will not be extensive and will serve to clarify points of ambiguity.

LOCATING ANCHOR PAPERS

As a final step in rubric design, samples of student work that represent different points on the scale on each of the different criteria should be identified. By keeping these from year to year, it is possible to chart the course of general improvement of student work over time. In addition, only through the use of anchor papers can educators be sure that their standards are remaining the same, and are not subject to a gradual drift.

SUMMARY

Not until a scoring rubric has been piloted with actual student papers will its designers know whether it will prove to be effective.

INVOLVING STUDENTS IN RUBRIC DESIGN AND USE

Many educators find that one of the most powerful uses of performance tasks and rubrics is to engage students actively in their design and use. That aspect of work with rubrics is described in this section.

ADVANTAGES

Many advantages are cited for engaging students in the design of scoring rubrics. First and most important, by participating in the design of a scoring rubric, students are absolutely clear on the criteria by which their work will be evaluated. Furthermore, many teachers discover that students have good ideas to contribute to a rubric; they know, for example, the characteristics of an exemplary mathematics project.

But more importantly, when students know at the outset the criteria by which their work will be evaluated, and when they know the description of exemplary performance, they are better able (and more motivated) to produce high-quality work. The rubric provides guidance as to quality; students know exactly what they must do.

Consequently, many teachers find that when they involve students in the use of scoring rubrics, the quality of student work improves dramatically. So, when teachers have anchors (e.g., exemplary projects from a previous year) to illustrate good quality work to students, the general standard of work produced improves from year to year.

A PLAN FOR ACTION

It is not obvious just how to engage students in designing and using scoring rubrics for evaluating student work. Some suggestions are offered here.

- *Starting with a draft.* A discussion with students about scoring rubrics should begin with a draft rubric already prepared by the teacher. The teacher should have some ideas, at least in general terms, of the criteria that should emerge from the discussion. Then, while students may suggest original ideas, the teacher can be sure that the final product includes all important aspects of performance.

Students may be asked to contribute both to the generation of criteria and to the writing of performance descriptions. Many teachers are pleasantly surprised with the level of sophistication demonstrated by their students in this endeavor.

The teacher should maintain control of the process of rubric design. While students will have excellent ideas, which should be accommodated to the maximum extent possible, the teacher should never relinquish control of the project to students.

* *Student self-assessment.* The first type of student use of a scoring rubric should be for students to evaluate their own work. Most teachers find that their students are, generally speaking, quite hard on themselves, in some cases more so than their teachers would be. Of course, clear performance descriptions will help in keeping evaluations consistent, but students frequently reveal a genuine concern for maintaining high standards, even when evaluating their own work.

* *Peer assessment.* When the climate in a class is sufficiently supportive, students may be able to engage in peer assessment. Such an activity requires a high level of trust among students. However, if students have participated in the design of a scoring rubric, and have used it to evaluate their own work, they will generally be able to provide feedback to their peers in the same spirit of caring and support. When that occurs, the classroom becomes transformed into a true community of learners.

SUMMARY

The most powerful use of scoring rubrics derives from engaging students in their design and use. However, such participation by students is likely to evolve over time.

7

ADAPTING EXISTING PERFORMANCE TASKS AND RUBRICS

Frequently, much time and effort may be saved by adapting an existing task, with its scoring rubric, to one's own use. Through this approach, educators can benefit from the work of others, and still have a task that reflects their own unique needs.

There are many sources of existing performance tasks that may be adapted, in addition to those in this book. Many textbook publishers now offer some performance tasks and rubrics as part of their package. Some state departments of education have also created prototype tasks. And the National Council of Teachers of Mathematics (NCTM) has published some examples. The techniques for adapting existing tasks are described in this section.

MATCHING OUTCOMES, TOPICS, AND STUDENTS

The first step in identifying tasks suitable for adaptation is to match the outcomes and topics assessed by the task with those in one's own curriculum. The performance tasks in this book have been aligned with the strands developed by the New Standards Project, and with different topics found in most mathematics curricula. By examining those alignments, educators can determine whether a given task would be of value to them in assessing student mastery of their own curriculum.

It is unlikely that such a match will be perfect. Frequently, a performance task will ask students to perform an operation or complete an activity that students in a given class have not yet learned. Alternatively, a scoring rubric will include criteria that do not reflect a district's curriculum. In those cases, either the task or the rubric will have to be adjusted.

Also, a particular task might have been developed with students in mind who are very different from one's own class. In order for a task to be effective, it must be one that students can relate to.

SUMMARY

In order to determine whether a performance task can be used as written, educators must match the task's outcomes and topics with those in their curriculum, and consider their own students.

ADJUSTING THE TASK

The actual task may need adaptation, either to reflect a school's curriculum, to make it more meaningful and relevant to the students concerned, or to adjust the situation to local conditions. Each of these situations will be considered separately in this section.

TO REFLECT A SCHOOL'S CURRICULUM

If there is poor alignment between a performance task and a school's curriculum, the task must be adjusted to correct the mismatch. Such an adjustment will take the form of adding to or subtracting from, or simply changing, the requirements for the students. For example, a particular task might require students to find an average of a group of numbers as one step in solving a problem. If students in a particular class have not yet learned how to do that, the task should be adjusted so that such a step is not needed.

Alternatively, one school's curriculum might teach estimation in the course of work in measurement, while a performance task involving measurement does not, as written, ask the students to estimate their answer before measuring and calculating. In that case, adapting the task might involve adding a step which requires the students to estimate.

TO REFLECT A GROUP OF STUDENTS

Sometimes a task is designed with the characteristics of a group of students in mind, and it is not ideally suited to others. Different classes of students are not identical in the sophistication of their thinking, and in the knowledge and skills they bring to a class. Therefore, a performance task that is to be used with any group of students must be considered with the characteristics of that class in mind.

This factor will often be reflected in the amount of scaffolding provided to students as they solve problems. For lower-functioning students, a task might have to be written with more "tips" for solution than would be needed for more advanced students. Alternatively, a single task might be broken into several sub-tasks that students work on separately.

On the other hand, a task can be made more difficult and cognitively complex. A task that asks students simply to find an answer can be adjusted to require, in addition, an explanation of why a certain approach was employed. Or, a task that includes many suggestions for students as to how to proceed could be rewritten with just the question, with few or no "tips" to the student. Each of these efforts will make the task more challenging, and may make it suitable for an advanced group of students.

If a performance task is adjusted to reflect a group of students, particularly if it is deliberately made more or less challenging, it should be adapted purposefully and the changes noted when student progress is monitored. If, for example, a task is deliberately simplified for a group of students, it should be clear to any reader of those students' records that the curriculum outcomes on which they were evaluated were somewhat different from those of another group of students.

To Enhance Its Relevance

Another type of adaptation that might be warranted is that which makes a performance task more suitable to a local situation, and therefore more relevant and meaningful to a group of students. For example, a task might ask students to calculate the amount of money they could earn by recycling their household cans, bottles, and plastic containers. If, however, steel cans and plastic cannot be recycled in a particular area, it might be a good idea to revise the task so it concerns only aluminum cans and glass bottles.

Alternatively, an entire situation might be changed to reflect local conditions. For instance, a performance task might concern calculating the floor area of a school's classrooms for the purpose of recommending the purchase of carpeting. If, however, the school is about to have all its walls painted, the students could make those calculations instead, and actually make a presentation of their findings to the maintenance department of the school district. Such efforts to enhance relevance and authenticity pay big dividends in enhancing student engagement in the task.

Summary

A performance task may be adjusted to make it more reflective of the school's curriculum, or more suitable to a group of students, or to reflect conditions in a particular setting.

Adjusting the Rubric

If a task is adjusted to reflect a district's curriculum, to be more suitable to a group of students, or to be made more relevant, the rubric will probably also require adaptation. The extent to which such adaptation is needed will depend, of course, on the amount of adjustment to the task itself.

Adapting The Criteria

If the task is changed, the criteria may no longer apply. The task may now encourage students to exhibit knowledge, skill, or understanding that were not part of the original task. If so, criteria related to these features should be added. Alternatively, elements of the original task may have been dropped; if so, the criteria corresponding to those elements should be eliminated.

ADJUSTING THE PERFORMANCE DESCRIPTIONS

When a task is changed, particularly if the evaluation criteria are also changed, the performance descriptions may require adjustment. Occasionally, the performance descriptions need adjustment even with no change in the task itself.

* If the level of difficulty of a task has been changed, either by altering the cognitive demands of the directions or by splitting it into several discrete tasks, the performance descriptions for even the same criteria may no longer be suitable. The descriptions may require revision to reflect the changed demands of the revised task.

* Even if the task has not been changed, but is being used with students who are more or less advanced than those for whom it was designed, the performance descriptions may need revision. Sometimes this can be accomplished by simply shifting the descriptions one place to the right, or the left; that is, the description that was a "3" is now a "2," that which was a "4" is now the "3," and a new description is written for the "4."

* If the task has been revised to reflect a particular situation (for example, calculating floor area for carpeting instead of wall area for paint), the performance descriptions may need revising to reflect the changes. On the other hand, they may not need revision, depending on how they were written in the first place. Clearly, the more generic they are, the less revision will be needed. But if the rubric has been written to be highly task-specific, substantial changes will be needed to reflect a different context.

Summary

If a performance task is adjusted to make it more suitable for a group of students, its scoring rubric will almost certainly require a parallel change. Even if the task is not changed, educators may find that they want to adjust the rubric to better match the skills of their students, or the criteria important to them.

Piloting With Students

No adaptation of a performance task and its rubric is complete without trying it with students. Generally, all performance tasks (even those that are not adaptations of existing tasks) are revised somewhat after this pilot; certainly the scoring rubrics are revised in light of actual student work. The questions to be answered as a result of this pilot are summarized below.

Engagement and Authenticity

Are students engaged in the task? In the course of revision, did the task become irrelevant and boring to students? If possible, does the task reflect authentic applications of knowledge and skill?

Eliciting Desired Knowledge and Skill

Does the task, as revised, elicit the desired knowledge and skill from students? Occasionally, when tasks are revised, they lose their essential nature, so students complete the task without demonstrating the critical knowledge and skill about which their teachers are interested. This is most likely to happen if the student directions have been substantially revised.

Clarity of Student Directions

Are the directions to the students clear? In particular, if student's work will be evaluated according to specific criteria, have students been informed, in some manner, of those criteria in the directions themselves?

INDIVIDUAL ASSESSMENT

Does the task still permit the assessment of individual students? Or have the teachers, in the interests of making the task more relevant to a particular group of students or a unique situation, also introduced group work that obscures the contribution of individuals?

TECHNICAL FEATURES OF THE RUBRIC

Does the scoring rubric, as revised, still meet all the technical requirements described in Chapter 6? Do the descriptions of levels of performance use vivid words, and avoid comparative language? Are the distances between points on the scale approximately equal? Do the criteria reflect the most important aspects of performance?

Only an actual pilot of the revised task will elicit unambiguous answers to these questions. As educators and their students become more experienced in the use of performance tasks, however, this step may be combined with the first actual use of the task to evaluate student learning. That is, the task may be adapted as needed and used with students. Then, if it becomes apparent that the adaptation did not avoid all the pitfalls described above, the actual scores awarded to students can be adjusted accordingly. For example, if student performance is poor, but it becomes clear that the principal reason for the poor performance relates to lack of clarity in the directions, then the teacher's evaluation of student mastery must reflect that difficulty.

SUMMARY

The final step in adapting an existing performance task and rubric is its actual pilot with students. Only then can educators be sure that it accomplishes their desired purposes.

8

MIDDLE SCHOOL MATHEMATICS PERFORMANCE TASKS

In this section of the book you will find a collection of performance tasks and rubrics aligned to the mathematics standards, and addressing all the important topics in middle school mathematics. They are arranged in alphabetical order (by title), with a table at the beginning of the chapter to assist you in locating tasks you may want to assess specific skills and concepts. Some of the tasks include student work, which serves both to illustrate the manner in which students interpret the directions given to them and to anchor the different points in the scoring rubrics.

You may find that the tasks are useful to you as presented. Alternatively, you may find that they can serve your purposes better if you adapt them somewhat. One way of adapting tasks is to incorporate names of people and places familiar to students in your class. This practice is frequently amusing to students, and therefore engaging.

In addition, tasks may be simplified or made more difficult by increasing or decreasing the amount of structure (or scaffolding) you provide to students. When you, the teacher, give guidance to students by outlining the steps needed in a solution, the resulting task is significantly easier (and less authentic.) Similarly, for those tasks that are provided with considerable scaffolding, you can make them more complex by removing it.

Task \ Standard	Number Operations Computation	Geometry Measurement Dimension	Patterns Functions Algebra
All in a Day	X	X	
Basketball Camp	X		
Bull's Eye	X	X	X
Checkers			
Concession Stand	X		X
Country Mile	X	X	X
Cover it Up	X	X	
Day Care Center	X	X	X
Lineup	X		X
Locker Combinations	X		X
Lucky Soda	X		X
Money from Trash	X	X	X
Music Company	X		X
Name Game	X		X
Outfits	X		X
Pinhead	X	X	X
Pizza Party	X	X	X
Pool Pleasure	X	X	X
Popcorn Estimation	X	X	
Skydiving		X	
Spot	X		X
Traffic Lights			
TV Show			X
Variable Dilemma	X		

Statistics Probability	Reasoning, Problem Solving	Mathematical Skills and Tools	Math Communication
X	X	X	X
	X	X	X
X	X	X	X
	X	X	X
	X	X	X
	X	X	X
	X	X	X
	X	X	X
X	X	X	X
X	X	X	X
X	X	X	X
	X	X	X
X	X	X	X
X	X	X	X
X	X	X	X
X	X	X	X
	X	X	X
	X	X	X
	X	X	X
	X	X	X
	X	X	X
X	X	X	X
X	X	X	X
	X	X	X

ALL IN A DAY

MATHEMATICS STANDARDS ASSESSED

- Number operations and concepts
- Geometry and measurement
- Statistics and probability
- Problem solving and mathematical reasoning
- Mathematical skills and tools
- Mathematical communication

DIRECTIONS TO THE STUDENT

Make a graph to illustrate how many hours you spend on a typical school day involved in different types of activities. You should think about time sleeping, eating, being in school, doing homework, watching television, being with friends, playing sports, doing hobbies, etc.

You may want to make a table to organize your information, and you will have to select the best type of graph to use: for example, a bar graph, line graph, or circle graph. In addition, please show all your calculations and write a brief explanation of why you chose the graph you did and your method used in making the graph.

MATERIALS NEEDED

graph paper
ruler
compass and protractor (for a circle graph)
calculator

MATHEMATICAL CONCEPTS:

This task requests students to collect, analyze, and communicate information through a graph, table, or chart. They must first design a simple data table, and calculate the number of hours spent in a typical day in each of the major activities.

This activity will require that they estimate and calculate elapsed time. In addition, they should ensure that the number of hours in their "typical" day adds to 24 hours.

Next, students must select an appropriate graph or chart with which to communicate their results. A pictograph, a pie chart, and a bar graph are all suitable. A line graph would not be appropriate, since the events being graphed (sleeping, doing homework, eating, etc.) are discrete events; they are not continuous. For a circle graph, students will have to calculate the degrees of the circle represented by the different number of hours devoted to each activity.

Lastly, students must explain their method in writing. This narrative should reflect their estimation techniques, the reasons for their choice of graph type, and awareness that the sum of all the activities is 24 hours.

SOLUTION

Answers will vary, depending on students' daily routine. A possible solution, with the proportionate number of degrees in a circle graph, is presented below:

Activity	Number of hours	Degrees of a Circle
Eating	3 hours	45
Sleeping	8 hours	120
School	7 hours	105
Homework	2 hours	30
Bathing, dressing, etc.	2 hours	30
TV	2 hours	30
Total	**24 hours**	**360**

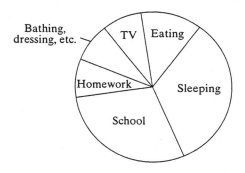

SCORING GUIDE

	Level One	Level Two	Level Three	Level Four
Organization of information	Information about time spent very disorganized.	Some data organization evident, but not carried through.	Data well organized.	In addition, the data is clearly presented.
Graph	Graph chosen is inappropriate to the topic or very poorly executed.	Graph chosen is adequate, but execution is poor.	Appropriate form of graph, and adequate execution.	In addition, the graph is very accurately and neatly presented.
Calculations	Major errors in calculations.	A number of small errors in calculations	Very few errors in calculations.	No calculation errors.
Explanation	Explanation very muddled.	Explanation difficult to follow.	Explanation clear enough to follow.	The explanation is very clear and displays comprehensive understanding of the relative merits of different types of graphs.

BASKETBALL CAMP

MATHEMATICS STANDARDS ASSESSED

• Number operations and concepts
• Problem solving and mathematical reasoning
• Mathematical skills and tools
• Mathematical communication

DIRECTIONS TO THE STUDENTS

Kristin won a 7-day scholarship worth $1000 to the Pro Shot Basketball Camp, but she will have to make some decisions about how to spend the money. Round trip travel expenses to the camp are $335 by air or $125 by train. At the camp she must choose between a week of individual instruction at $60 per day or a week of group instruction at $40 per day. Kristen's food and other living expenses are fixed at $45 per day. If she cannot add more money to the scholarship award, what are all the possible choices of travel and instruction plans that Kristen could afford to make?

Decide how you would recommed that Kristen spend her award, and write a brief letter to her explaining your thinking.

* This task is slightly adapted from one developed by the National Assessment of Educational Progress (NAEP) for its 1992 assessment.

MATHEMATICAL CONCEPTS

In this task, students must differentiate between fixed costs (living expenses) and variable expenses, and they must recognize that there are trade-offs to be made between different forms of travel and different forms of instruction. They must make accurate calculations and explain their thinking.

SOLUTION

Kristin's fixed expenses will be 7 x $45 or $315.00 for the 7 days. Therefore, she has $1000 - $315 or $685 to spend for travel and instruction. The group plan will cost 7 x $40 or $280 for the week while the individual plan will cost 7 x $60 or $420 for the week. Therefore, Kristin has three options:

Group instruction and train travel:	$280 + $125 = $405 with $280 remaining
Group instruction and plane travel:	$280 + $335 = $615 with $70 remaining
Individual instruction and train travel:	$420 + $125 = $545 with $140 remaining

Kristin does not have enough money to pay for individual instruction and plane travel since that would come to $420 + $335 or $755, $70 more than the $685 available after the fixed expenses are paid for.

SCORING GUIDE

	Level One	Level Two	Level Three	Level Four
Organization of Information	Information is disorganized.	Some attempt evident to organize the information, but only partially successful.	Organization of information is clear and reflects differentiation between fixed and variable expenses.	In addition, the information is highly organized and clearly presented.
Computational Accuracy	Major errors in calculation, resulting in erroneous conclusions.	Some computational errors, resulting in minor errors in conclusions.	Only minor computational errors; results are still correct.	No computational errors.
Letter of Explanation	Explanation is muddled and difficult to follow.	Intent of the explanation is fairly clear, but not well executed.	Explanation is clear.	In addition, the explanation reveals understanding of trade-offs.

BULL'S EYE

MATHEMATICS STANDARDS ASSESSED

- Number operations and concepts
- Geometry and measurement
- Functions and algebra
- Statistics and probability
- Problem solving and mathematical reasoning
- Mathematical skills and tools
- Mathematical communication

DIRECTIONS TO THE STUDENT

The archery target shown below is made of four circles, with radii of 1 foot, 2 feet, 3 feet, and 4 feet, and with points as marked. If you shoot an arrow at random at the target, and it does not miss the target altogether, what is the chance that you will earn a score of 10? What is the chance of earning a 7? a 5? a 3?

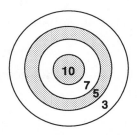

Write an explanation that a younger student could understand, describing how you arrived at your answers.

MATHEMATICAL CONCEPTS

In this task, students must apply concepts of geometry, proportions, and probability to calculate the chances of earning a score of 10, and each of the others. They must find the areas of the different concentric circles, or at least their ratios, to determine the likelihood of a randomly-shot arrow landing in each of the rings.

SOLUTION

The area of a circle may be found by applying the formula $a = \pi r^2$. The area of the smallest circle is 3.14 square feet (3.14 x 1 x 1). The most efficient way to solve the first problem is to recognize that the area of a circle varies in proportion to the square of the radius, and since the area of the entire dart board is 3.14 x 4 x 4, the chance of hitting a bull's eye is one chance in 16. Through calculation, one can demonstrate that the area of all the circles is 3.14 x 4 x 4 = 50.24 sq. ft., and that

$$\frac{3.14}{50.24} = \frac{1}{16} \text{ or } 6.25\%$$

As for the other scores, students must find the areas of each of the rings of the target. Using this approach, the area of the bull's eye circle is 3.14. The area of the next ring is 9.42 square feet [(3.14 x 2 x 2) - 3.14]. The area of the third ring is 15.70 square feet [(3.14 x 3 x 3) - (3.14 x 2 x 2)] or (28.26 - 12.56). The area of the outside ring is 31.40 square feet [(3.14 x 4 x 4) - (3.14 x 3 x 3)] or (50.24 - 28.26).

Therefore the ratio of the area of the second circle to the total area of all the circles is:

$$\frac{9.42}{50.24} = \frac{1}{5.3} = 18.75\%$$

The ratio of the area of the third circle to the total area of all the circles is:

$$\frac{15.70}{50.24} = \frac{1}{3.2} = 31.25\%$$

The ratio of the area of the outside circle to the total area of all the circles is:

$$\frac{21.98}{50.24} = \frac{1}{2.3} = 43.75\%$$

The answers may be checked by adding the probabilities of each of the rings, and determining that the sum is 100%. (6.25% + 18.75% + 31.25% + 43.75% = 100%).

There are many possibilities for error in this problem. Some students may believe that since the bull's eye circle has a radius of 1, while the largest circle has a radius of 4, that a randomly-shot arrow has one chance in four of hitting the center circle. Others may make errors in their calculations of the area of each of the rings, subtracting just the area of the next smaller ring, rather than the areas of all the previous rings.

SCORING GUIDE

	Level One	Level Two	Level Three	Level Four
Approach	Approach to the problem is disorganized, with no systematic approach.	Approach reveals some attempt at organization, but not completely carried through.	Approach is organized, and if followed would yield a correct solution.	The approach used is highly organized and systematic, with evidence of careful planning.
Computational Accuracy	Many errors in calculations, yielding wildly erroneous results.	Some computational inaccuracies, resulting in minor errors in the result.	Only minor errors in calculations; correct application of formulas.	No errors in computation; correct application of formulas and use of calculator.
Explanation of Procedure	Explanation unclear and difficult to follow.	Explanation is coherent, but reveals imperfect understanding of the problem.	Explanation is clear and reflects understanding of the problem.	In addition, the presentation is well structured to illustrate the relationship between the different rings.

CHECKERS TOURNAMENT

MATHEMATICS STANDARDS ASSESSED

- Problem-solving and mathematical reasoning
- Mathematical skills and tools
- Mathematical communication

DIRECTIONS TO THE STUDENT

Josh, Mike, Stacy, and Carrie have decided to organize a checkers tournament, with themselves as players. If they each play each of the others once only, how many games will be played?

Describe in words the method you used to figure out your answer. You may want to organize your information in a table or make some other 'picture' to represent the tournament.

As an extension, determine how many games would have to be played if a fifth student, and a sixth, were added to the tournament.

MATHEMATICAL CONCEPTS

This assessment task involves the number of different paired combinations of a small set of numbers. (This is somewhat different from a permutations problem, in that the game between Josh and Mike is the same as that between Mike and Josh.) The challenge for the student is to organize a method to identify all the possible combinations that is systematic and comprehensive. This is not difficult with a small number of competitors in the tournament, but only if the system is a good one will a student be able to extend it to a fifth and sixth competitor.

SOLUTION

Since there are four competitors in the tournament, each individual must play each other person, or three others. This may be illustrated by enumerating all the possible combinations, as, for example:

Josh - Mike
Josh - Stacy
Josh - Carrie
Mike - Stacy
Mike - Carrie
Stacy - Carrie

From this list, it is apparent that there are six games to be played. As other competitors are added, the list becomes correspondingly longer.

A more efficient method is to reason that since each individual must play a game with each other individual, the number of games to be played is 4 x 3 or 12. However, since this method counts permutations rather than combinations, it yields an answer that is double the correct answer. Therefore, the correct answer is 12 ÷ 2 or 6.

Hence, if another player is added, the number of games is 5 x 4 = 20 ÷ 2 = 10. For six players, the number of games is 6 x 5 = 30 ÷ 2 = 15.

SCORING GUIDE

	Level One	Level Two	Level Three	Level Four
Organization of information	Information randomly presented.	Some attempt to organize the information; however the system is ineffective.	Adequate organization of information in table or tree graph form.	In addition, the organization of information is highly systematic and neatly presented.
Accuracy	Findings are inaccurate, with major errors	Findings are inaccurate, with minor errors	Findings are accurate	In addition, the extension to five players is accurate.
Explanation	Explanation is not provided or is unclear.	Explanation reveals the intention of a systematic approach, but is not completely clear.	Explanation clearly describes a systematic approach.	The explanation is systematic and makes explicit recognition of a pattern.

SAMPLES OF STUDENT WORK

This problem presents an interesting challenge for students, and permits many possible ways to organize the information. Most students are able to find an approach to the problem, but very few are able to discern the generalized pattern, or make a systematic extension to more players in the tournament.

LEVEL ONE

	Josh	Mike	Stacy	Carrie	Ken
Josh		✓	✓	✓	✓
Mike	✓		✓	✓	✓
Stacy	✓	✓		✓	✓
Carrie	✓	✓	✓		✓
Ken	✓	✓	✓	✓	

To figure out this problem I put the names on the tops and side of the paper. I put lines through the paper to make twenty-five boxes. When I put check in the boxes it meant that Josh, Mike, Stacy, Carrie, and Ken set ups someone elses set of checkers. As you read on this chart I came up with twenty $\frac{2}{2}$ check

---

This response organizes the information in a rudimentary manner. However, the student fails to recognize that given this approach, each student would play every other student twice. Furthermore, the response gives no actual answer to the question.

LEVEL TWO

Josh*	Mike*	Stacy*	Carrie⊕	Ken°
Mike*	Stacy*	Carrie	Ken	
Stacy*	Carrie⊕	Ken		
Carrie⊕	Ken			
Ken°				

What I did was I made a chart and put the five names on the side. I then matched up all the names together. I also made sure that the children only played each other once. So, Josh played first, he played Mike, then he played Stacy, then Carrie, and last, but not least he played Ken. Now it is Mike's turn. Mike first plays Stacy, then he played Carrie, and last played Ken. Mike does not play Josh again. It's Stacy's turn. Stacy she played Carrie, then she played Ken. But, Stacy doesn't play Ken, Josh. Now it is Carrie's turn. She can only play Ken. Sh can not play Stacy, Mike, but Josh. Now it is Ken't turn. Now it is Ken't turn, but he can't play anyone, because he has already played them all. What is how I organized my chart.

This response organizes the information adequately, but gives no answer to the question. Furthermore, the student appears to confuse the sequence of organizing the information with the sequence of play in a tournament.

LEVEL TWO

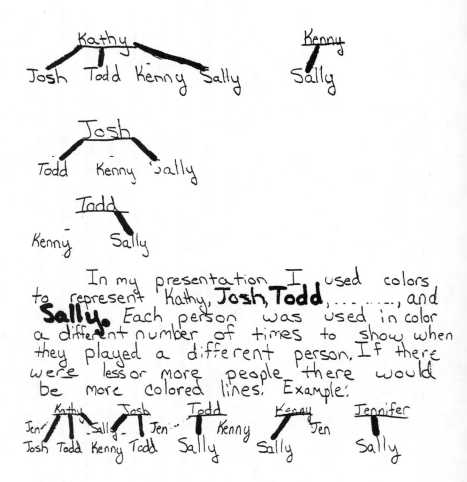

In my presentation I used colors to represent Kathy, **Josh, Todd**, ..., and **Sally.** Each person was used in color a different number of times to show when they played a different person. If there were less or more people there would be more colored lines. Example:

This response provides no answer to the question and the explanation is difficult to follow. However, the student appears to understand the situation and the organization would be adequate to solve the problem.

LEVEL THREE

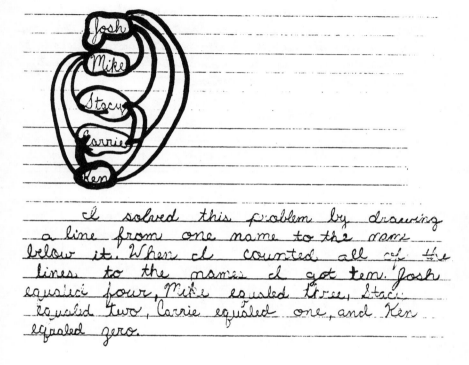

  I solved this problem by drawing a line from one name to the name below it. When I counted all of the lines to the names I got ten. Josh equaled four, Mike equaled three, Stacy equaled two, Carrie equaled one, and Ken equaled zero.

This response is rated a 3-. It accurately organizes the information and provides an explanation that is fairly clear.

LEVEL THREE

How I organized my chart is that I put the word "Play" so that the person that might read this would know who played who. I also put the words "Already Pl." so that the person would know that that person already played the other people or person.

Answer: 10 plays

Josh	Mike	Stacy	Carrie	Kenny

Play
1. Josh,
  Mike
	Play
	5. Mike,
	  Stacy
		Play
		8. Stacy,
		  Carrie
			Play
			10. Carrie,
			  Kenny
			Already Pl.
				Already P
				Carrie
				Stacy
				Mike

2. Josh,
  Stacy
	6. Mike,
	  Carrie
		9. Stacy,
		  Kenny
		Already Pl.
			Stacy
			Mike
			Josh
				Josh

3. Josh,
  Carrie
	7. Mike,
	  Kenny
	Already Pl.
		Mike
		Josh		

4. Josh, Kenny	Josh			

This response provides the correct answer to the question using a well-organized approach. The explanation is clear.

LEVEL THREE

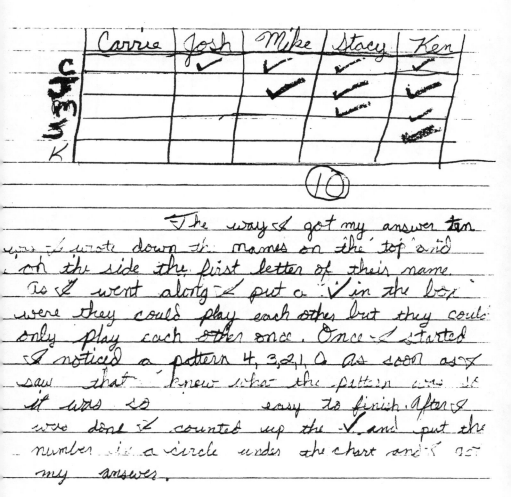

The way I got my answer ten
was I wrote down the names on the top and
on the side the first letter of their name.
As I went along I put a √ in the box
were they could play each other but they could
only play each other once. Once I started
I noticed a pattern 4, 3, 2, 1, 0 as soon as I
saw that I knew what the pattern was if
it was so easy to finish. After I
was done I counted up the √ and put the
number in a circle under the chart and I got
my answer.

This response is rated a 3+. The information is clear but not very neatly presented. However, the response makes explicit recognition that the situation can be efficiently solved through applying a pattern.

Level Four

Josh	Kathy	Todd	Kenny	Sally
Josh, Kathy	Kathy, Todd	Todd, Kenny	Kenny, Sally	Sally was
Josh, Todd	Kathy, Kenny	Todd, Sally		mentioned
Josh, Kenny	Kathy, Sally			three tim...
Josh, Sally				before +
				has no
				one to
				play.

$$4 + 3 = 7 + 2 = 9 + 1 = 10$$

10 games will be played

The way I figuerd this out was I made
a chart having each player play another player
1 time. When I was finished doing that I added
up and got my answer of 10.

extended

Josh	Kathy	Todd	Kenny	Sally	Mar...
Josh, Kathy	Kathy, Todd	Todd, Ken	Ken, Sally	Sally Mary	Again
Josh, Todd	Kathy, Kenny	Todd, Sally	Ken, Mary		Mary
Josh, Ken	Kath, Sally	Todd, Mary			was
Josh, Sally	Kathy, Mary				playe...
Josh, Mary					befc...

15 games $5 + 4 = 9 + 3 = 12 + 2 + 1 = 15$ 64

This response is rated a 4- because, while it provides a correct
answer to the basic question and to the extension, it makes no
explicit recognition of a pattern in the information.

CONCESSION STAND

MATHEMATICS STANDARDS ASSESSED

- Number operations and concepts
- Functions and algebra
- Problem solving and mathematical reasoning
- Mathematical skills and tools
- Mathematical communication

DIRECTIONS TO THE STUDENT

You are in charge of scheduling people to work in the concession stand at the state-wide soccer tournament for the next two weekends. Create a schedule that will satisfy the guidelines below and present it in an organized manner, both to the owner of the stand and to each of the workers.

GUIDELINES

1. The concession stand is open from 9 a.m. to 7 p.m. on the two Saturdays, and from 11 a.m. to 5 p.m. on the two Sundays.

2. There may be one, two, or three people working in the stand at any one time, depending on how busy you think the stand will be.

3. You can pay workers $4.25 per hour; workers should work no more than one shift per day.

4. Your total budget for paying workers for the four days is $350.00, although you don't have to spend it all.

5. If possible, in their different shifts, people should work with different co-workers; every worker does not have to work each day.

Your completed work will include:

- A schedule for the four days (two Saturdays and two Sundays) with the shifts identified, and the number of workers for each shift. For example, you can arrange 1-hour shifts, 2-hour shifts, 3-hour shifts, 4-hour shifts, or some combination of these.

- The number of workers for each shift, reflecting how busy you think the concession stand will be.

- The total number of workers you will need.

- A budget for paying the workers.

- A written description of why you think your schedule is a good one.

MATHEMATICAL CONCEPTS

In this task, students are required to organize complex information, working within a set budget, recognizing various trade-offs.

SOLUTION

There are many possible solutions to this problem. A possible solution is presented below.

Shift	Number of workers: Saturday	Number of workers: Sunday	Person-hours	Rate per hour	Total Pay	Total for both weekends
9-11	2	-	4	$4.25	$17.00	$34.00
11-1	3	3	12	$4.25	$51.00	$102.00
1-3	2	2	8	$4.25	$34.00	$68.00
3-5	3	2	10	$4.25	$42.50	$85.00
5-7	3	-	6	$4.25	$25.50	$51.00
Total	13	7				$340.00

SCORING GUIDE

	Level One	Level Two	Level Three	Level Four
Organization and Planning	No organization or plan in evidence.	A rudimentary plan used, but inadequate to the complexity of the situation.	Information is organized and plan is used to create a schedule.	Organization and planning reflect a highly systematic approach.
Mathematical Accuracy	Many computational errors made.	Some computational errors, but allowing largely for accurate conclusions.	Virtually no computational errors, with accurate conclusions.	In addition, the schedules and budget reflect reasonable assumptions about the situation.
Explanation	Little or no explanation, or impossible to follow.	Explanation attempted, but difficult to follow.	Explanation fairly clear, but thinking processes not always easy to follow.	Explanation very clear, and thinking processes easy to follow.

COUNTRY MILE

MATHEMATICS STANDARDS ASSESSED

- Number operations and concepts
- Geometry and measurement
- Functions and algebra
- Problem solving and mathematical reasoning
- Mathematical skills and tools
- Mathematical communication

DIRECTIONS TO THE STUDENT

In an old folk tale, a poor peasant is offered as much land as he can walk around from sunup to sundown. If you were given that offer, how much land could you claim? What shape would it be?

In order to answer these questions, you may want to:

- Determine the length of a day from sunup to sundown. Is it the same every day? At which time of year would you choose to make your walk?

- Determine how fast you can walk in an hour, and how many hours you could walk in the day. You should consider the need for food and rest during the day.

- Determine the best shape to walk around to claim the most land. Will it be a square? Some other rectangle? A circle? Some other shape?

- Calculate the amount of land (in square miles) that you could claim.

Your answer should include:

- Drawings of the different possible shapes you might use, with their respective areas and perimeters

- A clear presentation of the methods you used to calculate:
  - the length of the day

- the distance you can walk
- the area you can claim
• All work should be clearly labeled.

MATHEMATICAL CONCEPTS

This assessment task involves the relationship between area and perimeter, and the fact that for a given perimeter, the largest enclosed area is a circle. Of the rectangular shapes, a square encloses more area than a rectangle. However, in addition, the task requires students to demonstrate many other skills and perform many mathematical manipulations, including:

• knowing that the longest day of the year is at the summer solstice, and approximating how many hours of daylight there are at that time,

• determining how fast s/he can walk in an hour, possibly by measuring the distance that can be walked in 15 minutes, and extending that to an hour,

• estimating the amount of time needed for meals, rests, etc.,

• calculating the distance that can be walked in a day and the area enclosed,

• making clear drawings of the different possible shapes, and

• writing a clear description of the process used.

As written, this task presents extensive "scaffolding" through the bulleted list of steps to be used in solving it. It could be given to students without those hints, making it correspondingly more difficult.

SOLUTION

Answers will vary, depending on the assumptions made, but here is one possibility:

At the summer solstice, it is light from approximately 5 am to 9 p.m., an elapsed time of 16 hours. A person would need to rest for about 2 hours in that time, leaving 14 hours for walking (assuming a high level of physical fitness.) If one were able to walk on roads, one could walk about 3 miles per hour, or 42 miles in the course of the 14 hours. If one had to walk across fields, the rate would be more like 2 miles per hour at most, or 28 miles during the 14 hours.

If one walked on roads, the most efficient shape would be a square, with a side of 10.5 miles, and an area of 110 square miles. If one walked through fields, and could make a circle, the rate of 2 miles per hour would allow for a circumference of 28 miles, a diameter of 8.9 miles, a radius of 4.5 miles, and an area of 63.7 square miles. If, on the other hand, it were possible to maintain the same 3 miles per hour rate walking across fields, and one could walk 42 miles in a circle, the enclosed area would have a circumference of 42 miles, a diameter of 13.4 miles, a radius of 6.7 miles, and an area of 141 square miles. Hence, the rate one can walk is the most important factor affecting the amount of area that could be claimed.

SCORING GUIDE

	Level One	Level Two	Level Three	Level Four
Drawings of Shapes	No drawings provided or no attempt to determine the relative areas for shapes of the same perimeter.	Drawings of shapes reveal an attempt to analyze different shapes, but they include substantive errors.	Drawings of shapes indicate nalysis of area and perimeter but executed with minor errors.	Drawings of shapes indicate careful nalysis of shapes and their areas and perimeters..
Computational accuracy **- length of day** **- distance walked** **- perimeter of different shapes** **- calculation of areas** **- conversion to acres**	No systematic approach to making calculations; many computational errors.	Clear attempt at devising a systematic approach; however, it is ineffective; many computational errors.	Approach to organizing the computation is well designed; few errors.	Elegant and highly organized approach to completing the computations; no errors, and all work clear.
Overall Approach	Random and disorganized; no systematic approach.	Some system apparent in the approach; however, it is difficult to follow.	Systematic and organized approach, but not well presented.	Highly systematic and organized approach; neatly and clearly presented.

COVER IT UP

MATHEMATICS STANDARDS ASSESSED

- Number operations and concepts
- Geometry and measurement
- Problem solving and mathematical reasoning
- Mathematical skills and tools
- Mathematical communication

DIRECTIONS TO THE STUDENT

You are the president of a small painting company that is hoping to win the contract to paint the walls of your math classroom, using two coats of paint. In order to prepare your bid, you need to determine what the paint will cost. Calculate the number of cans of paint that will be needed, and their cost if you were to buy them from a paint store in your area.

In order to find the cost of the paint, you will need to:

- Measure and calculate the area of the walls in your math classroom,

- Determine how much area a single can of paint will cover (this is usually stated on the can itself),

- Calculate the number of cans required for two coats of paint,

- Calculate the amount the paint will cost,

Describe in words how you found your solution.

You may want to draw a diagram of the classroom. You should show all your work, and present it in a form that is neat and clear to read.

MATHEMATICAL CONCEPTS

This assessment task requires that students apply skills in measurement and calculation to a practical situation. They must measure with a reasonable degree of accuracy, and remember to exclude the doors and windows from their measurements. In addition, they must ensure that their measurements and those given on the paint cans, are in the same units, for example square feet. Lastly, they must calculate the amount of paint they will need (bearing in mind that they cannot purchase fractions of a can), and its cost.

SOLUTION

Solutions will vary, depending on the size and shape of the classroom and the type of paint available in the neighborhood. It is possible that you will have to supply the students with information from a paint can label for them to do the task. However, it is preferable for the students to locate that information themselves.

The steps in the solution should be clearly shown, and should include the following:

- calculations of the area of the walls of the classroom (preferably with a diagram to illustrate) that clearly exclude the windows and doors, and are performed to a reasonable degree of accuracy,

- information from a can of paint regarding the area that can be covered by the paint in a single can,

- calculations regarding the number of cans of paint that will be needed, and the total cost of the paint,

- a clear explanation of how the problem was approached, and how the answers were calculated.

SCORING GUIDE

	Level One	Level Two	Level Three	Level Four
Measurement Skills	Many errors in measurement, yielding incorrect calculations of area.	Minor errors in measurement, or minor confusion of units.	Few or no measurement errors, and correct units used.	Efficient system of measurement used, with evidence of thinking ahead.
Mathematical Accuracy	Inappropriate operation(s) selected, and/or many errors, leading to wildly erroneous conclusions.	Mixture of appropriate and inappropriate operation(s); some errors, but allowing largely for accurate conclusions.	Appropriate operation(s) selected; virtually no mathematical errors; with accurate conclusions.	In addition, the work shows evidence of advanced planning.
Approach	Random and disorganized; no systematic approach.	Some system apparent in the approach; however, it is difficult to follow.	Systematic and organized approach, but not well presented.	Highly systematic and organized approach; neatly and clearly presented.
Explanation	Little or no explanation, or impossible to follow.	Explanation attempted, but difficult to understand.	Explanation fairly clear, but thinking process not always easy to follow.	Explanation very clear, and thinking process easy to follow.

DAY CARE CENTER

MATHEMATICS STANDARDS ASSESSED

- Number operations and concepts
- Geometry and measurement
- Functions and algebra
- Problem solving and mathematical reasoning
- Mathematical skills and tools
- Mathematical communication

DIRECTIONS TO THE STUDENT

You have been hired by a day care agency to fence in an area to be used for a playground. You have been provided with 60 feet of fencing (in 4-foot sections), and a 4-foot gate. How can you put up the fence so the children have the maximum amount of space in which to play?

Try several different shapes that can be made with the fencing and calculate their areas. Include pictures of these shapes, drawing them roughly to scale. In addition, write a brief summary that describes which shape you think will have the largest area and why.

For an additional challenge, imagine that the fencing is flexible, and can be made to bend. What shape would have the greatest area and why?

MATHEMATICAL CONCEPTS

This assessment task concerns the relationship of area and perimeter. For a given perimeter, as the shape enclosed approximates a circle, the area increases. For example, a yard shaped as a skinny rectangle would use a lot of fencing for a small area. If the same amount of fencing were used to make a yard in the shape of a square, the area would be larger, and if it were made into an octagon the area would be larger still. Moreover, a circle would produce the largest area for the amount of fencing.

SOLUTION

The amount of fencing, including the 4' gate, is 64 feet. Since it is in 4 foot sections, the only rectangles that can be made with it are:

28' x 4' with an area of 112 square feet
24' x 8' with an area of 192 square feet
20' x 12' with an area of 240 square feet
16' x 16' with an area of 256 square feet.

A circle, on the other hand, made with the same amount of fencing, contains much more area. The formula for the relationship between the circumference and the diameter (or radius) is $C = \pi D$ or $C = 2 \pi r$. Therefore, the radius = the circumference divided by 2 x pi, or 64 divided by 2 x 3.14. The radius then is 10.2 feet.

The formula for the area of a circle is $a = \pi r^2$. With a radius of 10.2 feet, the area of a circle made with the fencing is 327 sq ft.

An octagon produces an area intermediate between that of a square and a circle. And if the fencing were made into other shapes, as the number of sides increases, approaching the shape of a circle, the area increases.

SCORING GUIDE

	Level One	Level Two	Level Three	Level Four
Approach	Approach is random; only one solution found.	Approach not very systematic, but several shapes are compared.	A systematic approach is possible to discern from the student work.	Highly systematic approach; well presented.
Accuracy	Many computational errors.	A number of computational errors and/or formulae improperly applied.	Very few computational errors; formulae correctly applied.	In addition, the work is neat and well presented.
Drawing	Sloppy and unclear; many errors.	Drawing is mostly clear; some errors in scale and/or labeling.	Drawing is clear and accurate, with the correct scale.	In addition, the drawing is neat and well presented.
Explanation	Unclear; no recognition of patterns in varying the area and perimeter.	Explanation hesitant; some recognition of patterns.	Clearly written; recognition of one aspect of relationship: number of sides or regularity..	In addition, recognition of both elements of relationship: number of sides and regularity.

LEVEL ONE

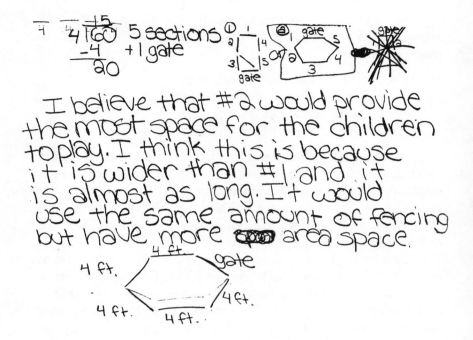

I believe that #2 would provide
the most space for the children
to play. I think this is because
it is wider than #1 and it
is almost as long. It would
use the same amount of fencing
but have more ~~area~~ area space.

This response offers no measurements nor calculations of area; the conclusion is the result of an "eye-ball" guess only. It does not appear that the student has fully understood the question.

LEVEL ONE

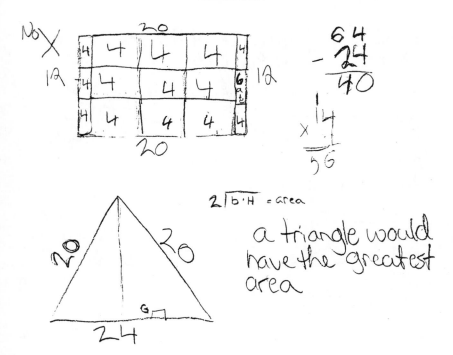

The student who submitted this response appears to be confused over the distinction between area and perimeter. While the dimensions of the rectangle and the triangle both measure 64 feet, their areas are not calculated correctly. Moreover, no other quadrilaterals are attempted (whose areas the student could probably determine) as a basis for comparison and for observing patterns.

LEVEL TWO

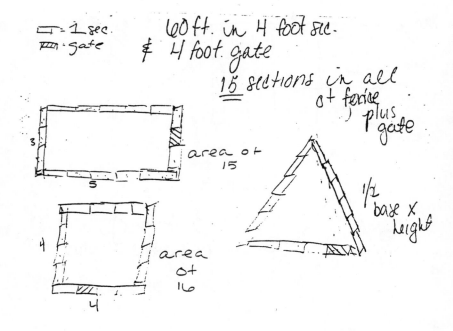

□ = 1 sec.
▥ = gate

60 ft. in 4 foot sec.
& 4 foot gate

15 sections in all
of fence
) plus
gate

area of
15

1/2
base x
height

area
of
16

In this response, several shapes are compared as to their area. However, no conclusion is drawn, nor is an explanation provided.

LEVEL TWO

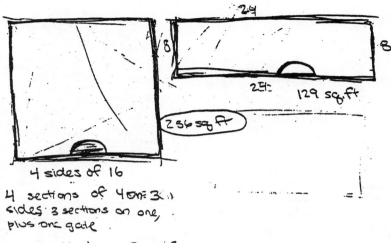

4 sides of 16

4 sections of 4 on 3
sides · 3 sections on one,
plus one gate

I believe that a simple
square of fencing is the best shape. Because the
kids have room side to side and front to back to
play in.

Challenge ( ) –If the gates were be nable, a
circle would be the best shape.

This is a 2+ response but not yet at the level of "3." It contains
an arithmetic or copying error, in that the area of one shape is
noted as "129" rather than "192 square feet." The correct conclusion is given, but with no rationale. The rectangular drawings are clear and roughly to scale, and the answers are given
in the proper units.

LEVEL THREE

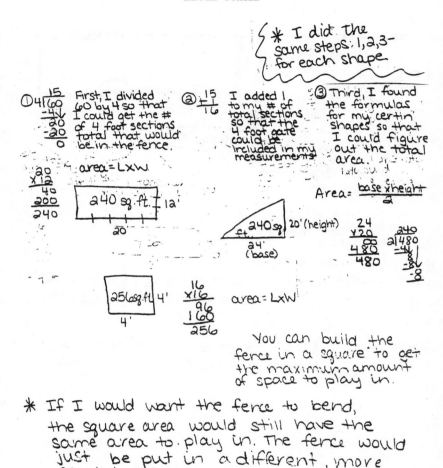

⌇ * I did the
same steps: 1,2,3-
for each shape.

① 4)60 ¹⁵ First, I divided
−4↓ 60 by 4 so that
−20 I could get the #
−20 of 4 foot sections
0 total that would
be in the fence.

② +1 ¹⁵ I added 1
16 to my # of
total sections
so that the
4 foot gate
could be
included in my
measurements.

③ Third, I found
the formulas
for my certin
shapes so that
I could figure
out the total
area.

20 area= LxW
×12
40
200
240

240 sq. ft.   12'
|‑‑‑‑|‑‑‑‑|
20'

Area= base x height
2

240 sq.
ft.   20' (height)
24'
(base)

24
×20
00
480
480

240
2)480
−4↓
08
−8

256 sq ft 4'   16
×16
96
160
256

area= LxW

4'

You can build the
fence in a square to get
the maximum amount
of space to play in.

* If I would want the fence to bend,
the square area would still have the
same area to play in. The fence would
just be put in a different, more
flexible shape.

This response is a solid "3." It provides a very clear explanation and correct conclusion for the square, and accurate calculations for the several shapes explored. However, the extension
to flexible fencing was not made correctly.

LEVEL THREE

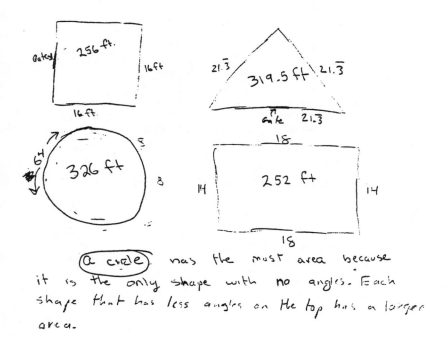

(a circle) was the most area because it is the only shape with no angles. Each shape that has less angles on the top has a larger area.

This response arrives at the correct answer and concludes that the circle is the shape with the largest area for its perimeter. However, the reason given (that "each shape that has less angles on the top has a larger area) is not accurate, and suggests less than complete understanding.

LEVEL FOUR

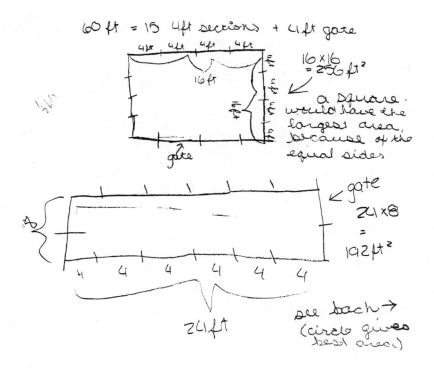

60 ft = 15 4ft sections + 4ft gate

4ft, 4ft, 4ft, 4ft

16 ft

16 × 16 = 256 ft²

a square would have the largest area, because of the equal sides

gate

gate

24 × 8 = 192 ft²

4   4   4   4   4   4

24 ft

see back →
(circle gives best area)

continued on next page

This response can be best evaluated as demonstrating the borderline between level three and level four. The student appears to understand the general principle that the closer a shape approaches a circle, the larger its area will be. However, the explanation is not very clear, nor is the presentation neat. The circle is not at all to scale.

LEVEL FOUR (CONTINUED)

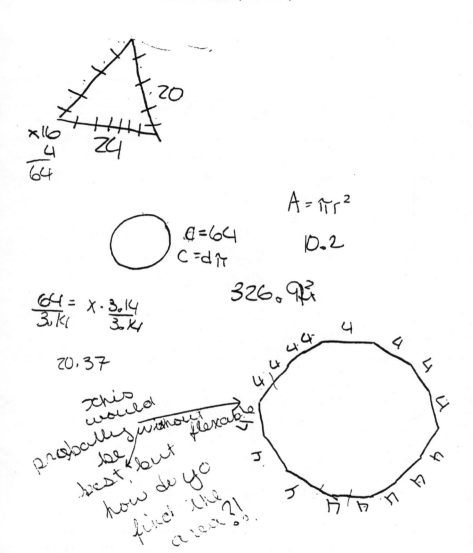

20

×16
4
——
64

24

$A = \pi r^2$

$A = 64$
$C = d\pi$

10.2

$\dfrac{64}{3.14} = X \cdot \dfrac{3.14}{3.14}$

$326.9\pi^2$

20.37

This would probaly be best, but without flexable, how do yo find the area?!

4 4 4 4
4
4
4
4
4
4
4
4
4
4

LEVEL FOUR

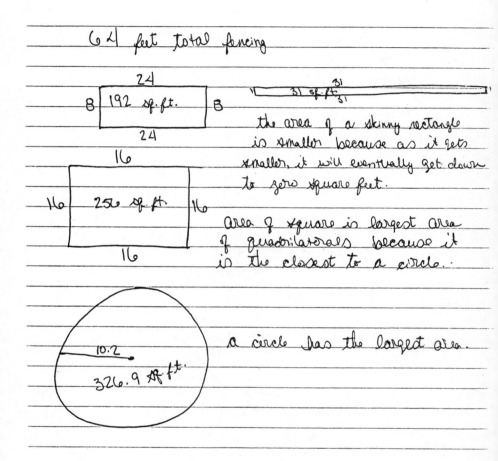

64 feet total fencing

24
B | 192 sq. ft. | B
24

31
31 sq. ft. 31

the area of a skinny rectangle is smaller because as it gets smaller, it will eventually get down to zero square feet.

16
16 | 256 sq. ft. | 16
16

area of square is largest area of quadrilaterals because it is the closest to a circle.

10.2
326.9 sq. ft.

a circle has the largest area.

This response is an example of a clear "4" on this task. The student not only arrives at the correct answer, but demonstrates understanding of the underlying mathematical principle, namely, that as shapes approach a circle their area increases and, conversely, that as rectangles become thinner and thinner (approaching a line) their area decreases to zero.

LINEUP

MATHEMATICS STANDARDS ASSESSED

- Number operations and concepts
- Functions and algebra
- Statistics and probability
- Problem solving and mathematical reasoning
- Mathematical skills and tools
- Mathematical communication

DIRECTIONS TO THE STUDENT

A baseball team has nine players; the order in which they bat is called the "batting order" or "lineup" For your school's baseball team, how many different lineups are possible? Write a brief description explaining your reasoning to the coach of the team.

MATHEMATICAL CONCEPTS

This task requires students to apply the concept of permutations to a practical situation. It may be used to introduce students to the concept of factorials.

SOLUTION

In a team with nine members, there are 362,880 possible lineups, a surprisingly high number. In order to solve the problem successfully, students will have to use a calculator. Students may approach the problem in several different ways; some possibilities are presented below:

- Students may analyze the number of possible lineups in a team with only 3 members, then 4, then 5, and discern the pattern. They may list these possibilities, or make them into a chart of some kind.

- Students may reason that any of the 9 members could bat in the first position, followed by any of the remaining 8 in the second position, any of the remaining 7 in the third position, and so forth.

An error that some students may make is to decide that the numbers should be added together, rather than multiplied. This would yield a total of 45.

SCORING GUIDE

	Level One	Level Two	Level Three	Level Four
Organization of information	Information randomly presented.	Some attempt to organize the information; however the system is ineffective.	Adequate organization of information in table or tree graph form.	In addition, the organization of information reveals understanding of the patterns.
Accuracy	Findings are inaccurate, with major errors	Findings are inaccurate, with minor errors	Findings are accurate	In addition, the calculations demonstrate understanding of the patterns inherent in the situation.
Description of procedure	Description reveals no understanding of a systematic approach	Description reveals limited understanding of a systematic approach, but incomplete.	Description adequately describes a systematic approach.	In addition, the explanation is efficient and clear.

LOCKER COMBINATIONS

MATHEMATICS STANDARDS ASSESSED

- Number operations and concepts
- Functions and algebra
- Statistics and probability
- Problem solving and mathematical reasoning
- Mathematical skills and tools
- Mathematical communication

DIRECTIONS TO THE STUDENT

Most school locker combination locks have 30 numbers on their dials, and a series of three numbers (right, left, right) opens the lock. If you forgot your combination, and decided to try all the possible combinations, how many would you have to try? How long do you think it might take you?

Write a brief explanation for your school newspaper explaining how safe you believe combination locks to be.

MATHEMATICAL CONCEPTS

In this task, students must apply the concept of permutations to a practical situation, and then integrate those findings with estimates regarding time.

SOLUTION

Answers will vary to some extent, depending on the assumptions made about time. But all answers should include reasoning such as the following:

- Since there are 30 numbers on the lock, and a series of three numbers makes up a combination, there are approximately 30 x 29 x 29 possible combinations, or 25,230. (The reason for the "29" rather than "30" in the equation is because a combination would not contain two identical numbers next to one another, such as 5-5-28. Some students may offer other such refinements.) If the school's locks have more or fewer numbers, the answers will be correspondingly different.

- In order to test all the possible combinations, one would need a systematic approach, so one could be sure of which ones had been tested. This would take some time to devise.

- It is possible to try a combination in about 15 seconds. Therefore, to test 25,230 combinations would require 6307 minutes, or about 105 hours. Since this is a considerable amount of time, it is likely that combination locks offer a fairly secure protection of students' belongings.

SCORING GUIDE

	Level One	Level Two	Level Three	Level Four
Organization of information	Information randomly presented.	Some attempt to organize the information; however the system is ineffective.	Adequate organization of information in table or tree graph form.	In addition, the organization of information reveals understanding of the patterns.
Accuracy	Findings are inaccurate, with major errors	Findings are inaccurate, with minor errors	Findings are accurate	In addition, the calculations demonstrate understanding of the patterns inherent in the problem.
Description of procedure	Description reveals no understanding of a systematic approach	Description reveals limited understanding of a systematic approach, but incomplete.	Description adequately describes a systematic approach.	In addition, the explanation is efficient and clear.

LUCKY SODA

MATHEMATICS STANDARDS ASSESSED

- Number operations and concepts
- Functions and algebra
- Statistics and probability
- Problem solving and mathematical reasoning
- Mathematical skills and tools
- Mathematical communication

DIRECTIONS TO THE STUDENTS

A soft drink company has hired you to help organize a promotion for its Cool Mist soft drink by including prizes in some of the bottles. The prizes will be tokens attached to the insides of the lids of the bottles; customers determine whether they have won by scratching the lids.

The soft drink company has created two types of prizes: "gold" awards and "silver" awards; the gold awards are $10.00 coupons for Cool Mist and the silver awards are $2.00 coupons. The company will put the prizes in 500 cases (12 bottles to a case) of soft drinks, but it needs a system to decide which bottles to put the winning lids on. They plan to award 25 gold prizes and 250 silver prizes, and they need a fair system for distributing them among all the bottles.

On the assembly line in the bottling plant, each bottle is assigned a number. Which bottles should be designated "gold" winners and which ones "silver" winners so the winning bottles are distributed through the entire 500 cases, and will therefore be distributed around the country? You should be sure that no bottle is assigned more than one prize.

To complete your job for the soft drink company, you should devise a method for awarding the gold and silver prizes such that:

- 25 gold prizes and 250 silver prizes are awarded

- no bottle has more than one prize

- the prizes are distributed evenly throughout the entire 500 cases

Write a brief letter to the president of the soft drink company, explaining which bottles should have the gold and silver prizes, and the method you used to determine the winning bottles.

MATHEMATICAL CONCEPTS

This task requires that students calculate the total number of bottles of soft drink to be produced, and then to distribute the 275 prizes evenly among them. It is primarily a task involving simple calculations, but a sequence for the calculations must be determined, and a system devised to ensure that no bottle is awarded more than one prize.

SOLUTION

Several approaches are possible for this problem, although they all start with determining the number of bottles of soda in 500 cases (500 x 12 = 6000), and numbering the bottles from 1 to 6000.

Step A: 6000 ÷ 250 = 24. Therefore, the silver prizes could be placed in one soda bottle of every 24, distributed throughout the 6000, for example, in bottles numbered: 24, 48, 72, 96, etc.

Step B: 6000 ÷ 25 = 240. Therefore, the gold prizes could be placed in one soda bottle of every 240, distributed throughout the 6000, for example, in bottles numbered: 240, 480, 720, 960, etc.

Step C: Since the bottles chosen for the gold prizes would have numbers that are divisible by 24, those silver prizes would have to be put in other bottles. Since there are 25 of those bottles, those silver prizes could be distributed throughout the 6000 bottles, possibly in the bottles immediately prior to the gold prizes.

An alternate approach would be to proceed from the fact that there are 275 prizes altogether (250 silver and 25 gold). The prizes could be placed in every 21st bottle, with 10 silver followed by one gold, this pattern repeated 25 times.

SCORING GUIDE

	Level One	Level Two	Level Three	Level Four
Approach	Random and disorganized; no systematic approach.	An attempt is made to use an organized approach; however, it is only partially successful.	Systematic and organized, but not well presented.	Highly systematic and organized, with clear presentation of method.
Mathematical Accuracy	Many mathematical errors, creating clearly wrong answers.	Some computational errors, but yielding essentially accurate answers.	Very few computational errors, with a solution that works.	All computations correct, and approached in a sophisticated manner.
Explanation	Little or no explanation, or impossible to follow.	Explanation attempted, but difficult to follow.	Explanation fairly clear, but thinking processes not always easy to understand.	Both explanation and thinking processes easy to follow.

MONEY FROM TRASH

MATHEMATICS STANDARDS ASSESSED

- Number operations and concepts
- Geometry and measurement
- Functions and algebra
- Problem solving and mathematical reasoning
- Mathematical skills and tools
- Mathematical communication

DIRECTIONS TO THE STUDENT

The eighth grade students at Washington Middle School are trying to raise money to help pay for a class trip. There are 250 students in the class, and they want to raise $2000.00 by recycling newspapers, cans, and glass and plastic bottles. Using the table below, calculate how many pounds of newspaper, cans, and bottles (or different combinations of these) students will have to collect to raise the money.

To complete this task:

- Determine how much each student is responsible to raise, and several ways students could fulfill their responsibilities.

- Based on the amount of newspaper, cans, and bottles your own family uses, decide which material you would collect for your contribution.

- Describe in words how you arrived at your conclusions.

MONEY FROM TRASH

Material	Amount per ton
Mixed paper	$40 per ton
Newspaper	$100 per ton
Aluminum cans	$1240 per ton
Steel cans	$50 per ton
Clear glass	$30 per ton
Green glass	-
Amber glass	$15 per ton
Plastic: soda bottles	$240 per ton
Plastic: milk bottles	$300 per ton

MATHEMATICAL CONCEPT

This task requires that students retrieve information from a table, make calculations using information from the table, collect information from their families, draw conclusions from information, and explain their reasoning in writing.

SOLUTION

With 250 students in the class, and $2000 to raise, each student must raise $8. According to the table, that $8 could be raised by recycling, for example, 160 lb. of newspaper, 13 lb. of aluminum cans, or 533 lb. of clear glass. Or, a student could raise the $8 through a combination of the different materials. Alternatively, students might elect to find another source of aluminum cans or newspapers, such as a Boys and Girls Club, or scout troop.

A complete table, showing the amount of each material worth $8.00, is presented on the next page:

Material	Amount per Ton	% ton worth $8.00	Number of pounds needed for $8.00
Mixed paper	$40	.20	400
Newspaper	$100	.08	160
Aluminum cans	$1240	.006	13
Steel cans	$50	.16	320
Clear glass	$30	.26	533
Amber glass	$15	.53	1067
Plastic soda bottles	$240	.03	67
Plastic mile bottles	$300	.026	53

Students will have to determine at least some of these calculations themselves, and incorporate them into their answer.

Students' narrative should show accurate reading of the original table, reasonable findings from the survey of home consumption, and should display awareness of the possible trade-offs involved. For example, a 32-ounce juice bottle weighs approximately 12 oz. If a student were to try to raise his or her share of the money by recycling only juice bottles, 710 of them would be needed.

SCORING GUIDE

	Level One	Level Two	Level Three	Level Four
Mathematical Accuracy	Many mathematical errors, leading to wildly erroneous conclusions.	Some errors, but allowing largely for accurate conclusions.	Virtually no mathematical errors; with accurate conclusions.	In addition, the work shows evidence of advanced planning.
Approach	Random and disorganized; no systematic approach.	Some system apparent in the approach; however, it is difficult to follow.	Systematic and organized approach, but not well presented.	Highly systematic and organized approach; neatly and clearly presented.
Explanation	Little or no explanation, or impossible to follow.	Explanation attempted, but difficult to understand.	Explanation fairly clear, but thinking process not always easy to follow..	Explanation very clear, and thinking process easy to follow.

MUSIC COMPANY

MATHEMATICS STANDARDS ASSESSED

- Number operations and concepts
- Functions and algebra
- Statistics and probability
- Problem solving and mathematical reasoning
- Mathematical skills and tools
- Mathematical communication

DIRECTIONS TO THE STUDENT

A music recording company is trying to decide which groups they should record on their label. They have asked you to help by determining which groups are most popular with students today, and which will be the most popular for several years. They have asked for your recommendations, supported by clear reasons.

In order to complete this job, you might:

- Determine students' favorite musical groups and ones which they think they will like in the next few years. This means that you must design a survey instrument of some kind.

- Conduct the survey of students.

- Analyze your data by organizing it into a table.

- Summarize your findings by making some type of graph or graphs.

- Calculate how many recordings could be sold to students in your entire school.

- Write a summary to the recording company, in which you recommend to them which artists they should record.

MATHEMATICAL CONCEPTS

This performance task requires students to design and conduct a survey of their peers, collect and analyze data, and communicate the results in both graphical and verbal form. It also asks students to write a persuasive "case" supporting the production of a certain vocal group.

SOLUTION

Answers will vary, according to the responses provided by the students.

SCORING GUIDE

	Level One	Level Two	Level Three	Level Four
Design of Survey Instrument	Questions very limited; will not serve to obtain necessary information.	Questions will elicit almost all information required for the task.	Questions will elicit all information required	In addition, questions asked in a manner to ease later data analysis.
Analysis of Data	Data poorly organized; hard to read and interpret.	Data organization is uneven.	Data organized but difficult to use for making a graph.	Data well organized and neatly presented.
Quality of Graph	Graph seriously flawed: inappropriate type, inaccurate, or error in execution.	Graph has one serious error	Graph is appropriate to the data, and is accurate.	In addition, the graph is well presented, with all details well executed.
Mathematical Projections	Mathematical projections inaccurate, with no apparent method used.	Although inaccurate, projections show evidence of a method being used.	Mathematical projections essentially accurate.	In addition, the mathematical projections are imaginative in their methodology.
"Case" Made to Producer	Ideas are not accurately summarized; a producer could not act on the findings.	Minor errors in the interpretation of findings.	Interpretation of data essentially accurate; data support findings.	In addition, the findings are presented in an imaginative manner.

NAME GAME

MATHEMATICS STANDARDS ASSESSED

- Number operations and concepts
- Functions and algebra
- Statistics and probability
- Problem solving and mathematical reasoning
- Mathematical skills and tools
- Mathematical communication

DIRECTIONS TO THE STUDENT

A sweatshirt company embroiders names on its sweatshirts; they charge customers for the service. It costs the company $.50 to embroider each letter, and they want to make 100% profit on the service. But they also want to charge a flat fee per name, rather than different amounts for different names. Most people want just their first name on their sweatshirt.

The company has asked you to advise them on the length of first names of young people so they can set a fair price for the embroidered names on the sweatshirts. How long is the average name? What could the company charge for an embroidered name that would enable them to make money overall?

In order to complete this task, you should:

- Determine a method to discover the length of first names,

- Collect and analyze sufficient data to make you confident of your results.

- Conclude a fair price for the sweatshirt company to charge for embroidering the names.

Write a letter to the president of the company with your recommendation for the price they should charge to embroider people's first names, and the method you used to determine your answer.

MATHEMATICAL CONCEPTS

In this task, students must design a method of statistical inquiry, dealing with issues of sample size, random selection, finding the mean, organizing and interpreting information, and evaluating conclusions.

SOLUTION

Solutions will vary, depending on the approach used by the student. However, two possible approaches are:

- Determining the number of letters in the names of students in the student's own class and extrapolating from that to the rest of the school and the larger universe of young people.

- Acquiring a listing of all the students in their class (for example, all the seventh graders), counting the number of letters in the names of students, graphing the results, and examining them to draw conclusions.

SCORING GUIDE

	Level One	Level Two	Level Three	Level Four
Mathematical Accuracy	Response indicates no idea of how to determine the average number of letters in students' names.	A clear attempt made to determine the average number of letters in students' names but minor errors.	Correct calculation of the average number of letters in students' names.	In addition, the method used to calculate is highly efficient.
Approach	No systematic approach to determining the average length of first names.	Some system is used but it is difficult to follow.	A system has been used to determine the number of letters, but with only a small sample.	An elegant system has been used to determine the number of letters in names, incorporating a large sample.
Organization and analysis of data.	Data poorly organized and analyzed.	Some attempt to organize the data, but many flaws or errors.	Adequate organization and analysis of data.	In addition, the organization and analysis is elegant and well presented.
Letter to the Company President	Conclusions invalid and methods used poorly explained.	Conclusions valid but methods used not clearly explained.	Conclusions valid and explanation clear.	In addition, the letter makes a strong case for the recommendations made.

OUTFITS

MATHEMATICS STANDARDS ASSESSED

- Number operations and concepts
- Functions and algebra
- Statistics and probability
- Problem solving and mathematical reasoning
- Mathematical skills and tools
- Mathematical communication

DIRECTIONS TO THE STUDENT

Maria is going to visit her cousins for the weekend. She packs a pair of purple pants, a pair of jeans, and a pair of blue shorts. For shirts she takes a blue tee-shirt, a white tank top, a yellow blouse, and a green shirt. In addition, she has three pairs of socks: white, yellow, and blue. How many different outfits can she make?

A picture or table will help you to organize the information.

Write a description of how you figured out your answer.

MATHEMATICAL CONCEPTS

This assessment task involves different combinations of a set of entities (in this case clothing.) Each day Maria will wear one top, one pair of either pants or shorts, and one pair of socks. Since she has four tops, three pants or shorts, and three pairs of socks, her outfits may be listed and counted. The challenge for the student is to use a systematic approach that will ensure that all the possibilities have been considered.

Note: for some students, considering only shirts and pants is a sufficient challenge. If desired, the task may be simplified in this manner.

SOLUTION

If the tops are assigned capitol letters (A, B, C, and D), the pants or shorts are assigned numbers (1, 2, and 3), and the socks are assigned small letters (a, b, and c), the outfits may be enumerated as A1a, A1b, A1c, A2a, A2b, A2c, A3a, A3b, A3c, B1a, B1b, B1c, B2a, B2b, B2c, B3a, B3b, B3c, C1a, C1b, C1c, C2a, C2b, C2c, C3a, C3b, C3c, and D1a, D1b, D1c, D2a, D2b, D2c, D3a, D3b, D3c. The total number of outfits is 4 x 3 x 3, or 36.

Many students will make a diagram to illustrate the situation, such as the following:

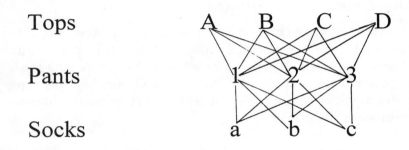

Tops

Pants

Socks

Alternatively, student might determine that for each top, there are 9 possible outfits. Since there are four different tops, the total number of possible outfits is 4 x 9, or 36.

SCORING GUIDE

	Level One	Level Two	Level Three	Level Four
Organization of information	Information randomly presented.	Some attempt to organize the information; however the system is ineffective.	Information is organized in a fairly systematic manner.	Organization of information shows recognition of the patterns inherent in the situation.
Method of Solution	Either no method used or method completely inappropriate.	Appropriate method used, but either not fully executed or possibly based on rote application only.	Appropriate method used, and likely to yield correct answer.	Method used highly elegant and efficient, revealing comprehensive understanding.
Accuracy	Findings are wildly inaccurate.	Solution is only slightly inaccurate, resulting from errors in counting or multiplying..	Solution is accurate, with a total of 36 outfits for Maria.	In addition, the calculations demonstrate understanding of the .structure of the problem.
Description of procedure	Description either missing or reveals an approach to the problem only by trial and error.	Description reveals limited attempt to use a systematic approach, but not entirely	Description adequately describes a systematic approach.	In addition, the explanation is efficient and clear, revealing complete understanding

LEVEL ONE

<u>Outfit 1</u>
Blue shorts
Blue T-shirt
Blue socks

<u>Outfit 2</u>
Purple Pants
White tank top
White socks

<u>out fit 3</u>
Jeans
green shirt
yellow socks

I listed everything that the girl had and I matched everything together randomly.

This response indicates no understanding of the concept of combinations, with three outfits formed randomly.

LEVEL ONE

pants	shirts	socks	shorts
purple	blexe	white	blue
blue	white	yellow	
	yellow	blue	
	green		

I used 2 to the power of N. N equals to 10.

$$2^{10} \frac{}{2N} \quad N=10$$

$$2 \times 2 \times 2 \times 2 \times 2 \times 2 \times 2 \times 2 \times 2 \times 2 = 1,024$$
$$4 \quad 8 \quad 16 \quad 32 \quad 64 \quad 128 \quad 256 \quad 512 \quad 1024$$

$$\begin{array}{cccccc} 32 & 64 & 128 & 256 & 512 \\ \times 2 & \times 2 & \times 2 & \times 2 & \times 2 \\ \hline 64 & 128 & 256 & 512 & 1024 \end{array}$$

In this response the student has applied a totally incorrect procedure, namely that of raising 2 to the power of 10. This student apparently recognizes that *something* must be done to the numbers to determine the combinations, and so applies an exotic approach.

LEVEL TWO

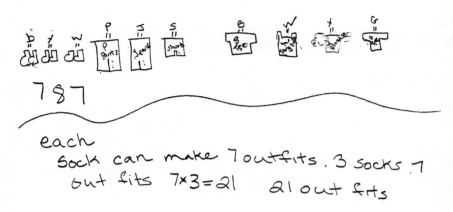

each
    Sock can make 7 outfits. 3 socks 7
    out fits 7×3=21   21 out fits

This response is a weak "2" because, while the student apparently recognizes the need for a systematic approach to solve the problem, the system itself is seriously flawed. The statement that "each sock can make 7 outfits" was presumably made because there are four tops and three types of pants, and that 4 + 3 = 7. This is incorrect: each pair of socks can be used to make 12 different outfits (4 x 3 = 12). However, the solution is not a random one, and reflects the recognition of a pattern.

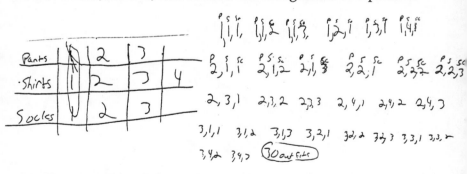

This response is a solid "2" with a reasonable approach to organizing the information. However, the student did not follow through with the system, resulting in an incorrect answer.

LEVEL THREE

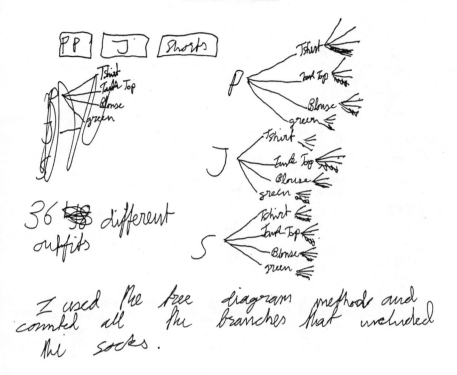

36 ~~38~~ different
outfits

I used the tree diagram method and
counted all the branches that included
the socks.

This response represents an accurate diagram of the situation,
and by counting, an accurate solution. However, the presentation is poor and the explanation is not fully elaborated.

LEVEL THREE

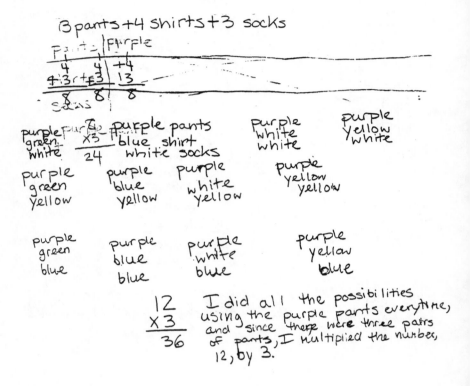

3 pants + 4 shirts + 3 socks

Pant = |Purple

4	4	+4
4·3r+£3	13
8	8	8
sдиз

purple purple purple pants   Purple   purple
green X3   blue shirt   white   yellow
white 24 white socks   white   white

purple   purple   purple   purple
green   blue   white   yellow
yellow   yellow   yellow   yellow

purple   purple   purple   purple
green   blue   white   yellow
blue   blue   blue   blue

12   I did all the possibilities
X3   using the purple pants everytime,
36   and since there were three pairs
      of pants, I multiplied the number,
      12, by 3.

In this response the student enumerated all the possibilities for
the purple pants and then multiplied the answer by 3. The system is not highly efficient or elegant; had it been, the solution
would have been a "4."

LEVEL FOUR

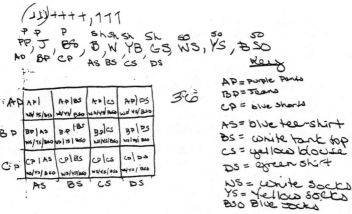

$(\underline{\cancel{JJ}})+++\,+\,,111$

? ? P sh sh sh SL so so so
PP, J, BS, B, W YB GS, WS, YS, BSO
AP, BP, CP, AS BS CS DS

Key

AP = Purple Pants
BD = Jeans
CP = blue shorts

AS = blue tee-shirt
BS = white tank top
CS = yellow blouse
DS = green shirt

NS = white socks
YS = Yellow socks
BSO Blue socks

3:6

AP	AP1	AP1BS	AP1cs	AP1DS
	ws/ys/bso	ws/ys/ bso	ws/ys/bso	ws/ ys/bso
BD	BP1AS	BP1BS	BD1cs	BP1DS
	ws/ys/bso	ws1ys1bso	ws/ys/bso	ws1ys1 bso
CP	CP1AS	CP1BS	co1cs	co1 Ds
	ws/ys/ bso	ws/ys/bso	ws/ys/bso	ws/ys/ bso
	AS	BS	CS	DS

I made a chart that showed the possible outfits
that can be made from Mana's vacationing
wardrobe. I put the pairs of pants on the
Y axis and the shirts on the x axis. I then added
3 pairs of sox to each combination box and
counted up to reach my answer.

In this response the student clearly understands the need for a systematic approach to the problem, and an organized structure to the data. The use of symbols for the different types of clothing is highly efficient, and the description of the procedure used reveals a clear understanding of the problem and its solution.

LEVEL FOUR

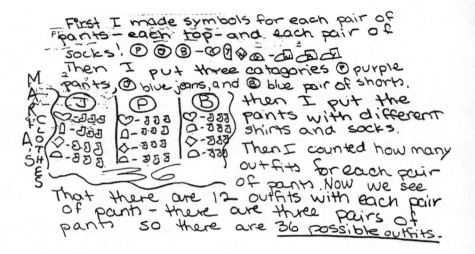

First I made symbols for each pair of pants — each top- and each pair of socks! Ⓟ Ⓖ Ⓑ - ♡§◊△ - ⬟⬠⬡

Then I put three catagories Ⓟ purple pants, Ⓖ blue jeans, and Ⓑ blue pair of shorts.

then I put the pants with different shirts and socks.

Then I counted how many outfits for each pair of pants. Now we see that there are 12 outfits with each pair of pants - there are three pairs of pants so there are 36 possible outfits.

This response also demonstrates a clear understanding of the structure of the problem and the type of organization needed to solve it successfully. The approach is well designed, and the symbols are clear, yielding an accurate solution.

PINHEAD? FAT-HEAD? IN-BETWEEN?

MATHEMATICS STANDARDS ASSESSED

- Number operations and concepts
- Geometry and measurement
- Functions and algebra
- Statistics and probability
- Problem solving and mathematical reasoning
- Mathematical skills and tools
- Mathematical communication

DIRECTIONS TO THE STUDENT

Do tall people have big heads? How could you find out? Investigate the relationship between height and size of head, and determine whether they are related. Summarize your findings in words and a graph of some kind.

As you decide how to answer this question, you might consider the following steps:

- Select a sample of people. This could be your own class, another class in your school, a group of people in your neighborhood, your soccer team or swim team, or any other group. Think about how large a group you need to draw any conclusions, and whether it matters if they are all students, or a combination of students and adults.

- Measure the height and head circumference of everyone in the group, using appropriate tools.

- Determine whether there is any relationship between height and the size of head, using any method you like.

- Present your findings, through a graph, table, chart, or any suitable approach.

- Write a brief summary of your investigation: how you went about it, what decisions you made, and what you found. Also include any additional questions you have as a result of your work.

MATHEMATICAL CONCEPTS

This task requires students to organize an investigation, collect data, organize and interpret their findings, and report their results. The relationship between height and head circumference could be expressed in any number of ways, from a table showing ratios to a line graph with points plotted. Students also must consider issues of size of sample, tools to use, and whether age is likely to make a difference in the results.

SOLUTION

Answers will vary, depending on the group chosen.

SCORING GUIDE

	Level One	Level Two	Level Three	Level Four
Design of Survey	No apparent recognition of the need to enlist a large sample.	Sample includes more than one type of group, e.g. students and adults.	Sample includes several types of population (students of different ages, adults.)	Survey organized to systematically separate the different populations.
Organization and Analysis of Data	Data poorly organized; hard to read and interpret.	Data organization and analysis is uneven; conclusions do not follow.	Data well organized and analyzed, but presented in a haphazard manner.	Data well organized and analyzed, and neatly presented.
Quality of Graph or Other Visual Representation	Representation seriously flawed: inappropriate type, inaccurate, or error in execution.	Representation has one serious error	Representation is appropriate to the data, and is accurate.	In addition, the graph or other representation is well executed, with attention to detail.
Explanation	Explanation is unclear and difficult to follow.	Explanation reveals only slight understanding of the issues involved.	Interpretation of data essentially accurate; data support findings.	In addition, the findings are presented in an imaginative manner.

PIZZA PARTY

MATHEMATICS STANDARDS ASSESSED

• Number operations and concepts
• Geometry and measurement
• Functions and algebra
• Problem solving and mathematical reasoning
• Mathematical skills and tools
• Mathematical communication

DIRECTIONS TO THE STUDENT

Your class has decided to have pizza for its end-of-the-year party. You are trying to decide which pizza store has the cheapest price. The local pizza stores and their prices are listed below.

Pizza Prices

Sam's Pizza House	$8.50, 8 slices per pizza
Pizza Palace	$10.25, 10 slices per pizza
Pizza & Stuff	$6.25, 6 slices per pizza

Assume that there are 30 students in your class and that each person (including your teacher) will eat two slices. Also, assume that the slices in the pizzas from the different stores are the same size. Where should you buy the pizza?

Please show all your work and write a brief description of how you decided on your answer.

MATHEMATICAL CONCEPTS

This performance assessment requires students to determine the best value for pizza. In this case they must consider both the number of pies needed from each source and the unit price per slice.

SOLUTION

Sam's Pizza House offers pizza at $8.50 for 8 slices. That comes to $1.06 per slice.

Pizza Palace offers pizza at $10.25 for 10 slices. That comes to $1.02 per slice.

Pizza & Stuff offers pizza at $6.25 for 6 slices. That comes to $1.04 per slice.

From this analysis it appears that Pizza Palace is the cheapest source of pizza. However, we must also consider the number of pizzas that must be purchased for each person to have two slices.

The class and the students together will eat 62 slices of pizza. That means they would have to buy:

8 pizzas from Sam's Pizza House for $68.00
7 pizzas from Pizza Palace for $71.75
11 pizzas from Pizza & Stuff for $68.75

Thus, it appears that the cheapest source of pizza, considering the number of pizzas that must be purchased, is Sam's Pizza House.

SCORING GUIDE

	Level One	Level Two	Level Three	Level Four
Strategy and Approach	Approach to the problem reveals no systematic strategy.	Approach to the problem reveals a rudimentary system, but not completely followed through.	Approach is systematic and will yield a correct answer.	In addition, the approach used is highly efficient, showing evidence of advanced planning.
Accuracy of Calculations	Many errors in calculations.	Minor errors in calculations.	Very few errors in calculations.	No errors, and evidence of efficient use of the calculator.
Written Description	Very little connection between the written work and the problem.	Written description shows evidence of following the plan, but poorly executed.	Written description clear and essentially accurate.	In addition, the written description shows evidence of complete understanding of the problem.
Presentation	Work not clear.	All work present, but difficult to follow.	Work is all present, and clearly presented.	In addition, the work is very well organized and neat.

POOL PLEASURE

MATHEMATICS STANDARDS ASSESSED

- Number operations and concepts
- Geometry and measurement
- Functions and algebra
- Problem solving and mathematical reasoning
- Mathematical skills and tools
- Mathematical communication

DIRECTIONS TO THE STUDENT

Your city Department of Recreation has finally obtained approval for the construction of a swimming pool and has requested your help with the design. The department would also like you to determine how much time it will take to fill the pool when it is built.

The pool will have to be able to hold 100 people and, in order for it not to be too crowded, you should allow 20 square feet of surface area per swimmer. The pool should be 3 feet deep in the shallow end and 9 feet deep in the deep end. You can make the shallow end as large as you like.

What are some possible shapes for the pool? Which do you like best? Which do you think would be the least expensive to build?

When the pool is built, how long will it take to fill? If the Recreation Department wants to open the pool on Memorial Day weekend (May 25), when should they begin filling it? The pipe they will be using can supply water at the rate of 6 gallons per minute, and a cubic foot of water contains 7.48 gallons.

Draw a picture of your pool and write a letter to the Director of Recreation to explain your recommendations.

MATHEMATICAL CONCEPTS

This task requires that students determine the minimum

area needed for the pool and possible dimensions to attain that area. They must also determine how much space to allow for the shallow end and the total volume contained by their design. Lastly, students must determine the time required for filling the pool, by converting rates of fill into hours and days needed.

SOLUTION

Solutions will vary, depending on the pool shape selected by the student. However, a possible solution follows:

A pool which will allow 20 square feet for each of 100 people must have at least 2,000 square feet. One way to have that is with a pool 40' x 50'. Two pictures of the pool, from a bird's eye view and from the side, are shown below:

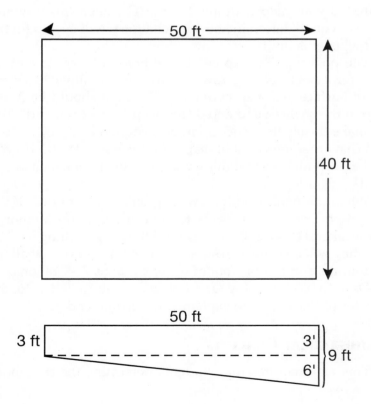

The volume of the pool is $(3 \times 40 \times 50) + \dfrac{6 \times 50 \times 40}{2}$ cubic feet or 12,000 cubic feet

At 7.48 gallons per cubic foot, there are 12,000 × 7.48 or 89,760 gallons in the pool.

To fill the pool with 89,760 gallons at 6 gallons per minute, 14,960 minutes are needed.

$\dfrac{14,960}{60}$ = 249.3 hours, or 10.4 days.

Therefore, the city should start filling the pool at least by May 14.

SCORING GUIDE

	Level One	Level Two	Level Three	Level Four
Mathematical Accuracy	Inappropriate operation(s) selected, and/or many errors, leading to wildly erroneous conclusions.	Mixture of appropriate and inappropriate operation(s); some errors, but allowing largely for accurate conclusions.	Appropriate operation(s) selected; virtually no mathematical errors; with accurate conclusions.	In addition, the work shows evidence of advanced planning.
Drawing of Pool	No drawing or sloppy; no attempt to show scale.	Drawing demonstrates attempt to represent the pool; however, not entirely clear.	Clear drawing of pool from one orientation; fairly clear as to shape and scale.	Drawing very clear, showing two views and clear sense of scale.
Approach	Random and disorganized; no systematic approach.	Some system apparent in the approach; however, it is difficult to follow.	Systematic and organized approach, but not well presented.	Highly systematic and organized approach; neatly and clearly presented.
Letter to the Recreation Department	Little or no explanation, or impossible to follow.	Explanation attempted, but difficult to understand.	Explanation fairly clear, but thinking process not always easy to follow.	Explanation very clear, and thinking process easy to follow.

POPCORN ESTIMATION

MATHEMATICS STANDARDS ASSESSED

- Number operations and concepts
- Problem solving and mathematical reasoning
- Mathematical skills and tools
- Mathematical communication

DIRECTIONS TO THE STUDENT

Estimate how many popcorn kernels there are in the container. You may use any of the materials in the classroom, including graph paper, scales, cups, rulers, calculators.

Explain your strategy and your reasoning. Think how you might verify your estimate.

MATERIALS NEEDED

- A large jar filled with popcorn kernels
- Cups of several different sizes, such as portion cups from a hospital, 7 oz cold drink cups
- Scales or pan balance and weights (standard or non-standard)
- Graph paper
- Calculators

MATHEMATICAL CONCEPTS

This assessment task requires that students devise a plan to estimate large numbers. It poses a challenge because the first response of most students — to simply count the kernels — is quickly discovered to be impossibly tedious. Therefore, students must create a strategy based on either area, volume, weight, or the successive dividing of numbers.

SOLUTION

Solutions will vary, depending on the size and capacity of the container chosen for the popcorn. In addition, student approaches will also vary considerably, and could include any of the following:

- Counting the number of kernels in a small cup, finding out how many small cups fit into a larger cup and multiplying the number of large cups filled by the number of kernels;

- Weighing a sample of kernels (subtracting the weight of the cup if appropriate), weighing the total number of kernels and dividing to discover how many cups of kernels are present in the total and multiplying that number by the number of kernels in one cup;

- Counting the number of kernels that covers a square unit of graph paper and multiplying that number by the total number of squares covered by all the kernels;

- Dividing the kernels in halves, quarters, eighths, etc., until a number small enough to count easily is achieved, and then reversing the process.

Because of the many different approaches to this problem, it is an excellent vehicle for exploring different strategies and comparing their relative merits. Do they yield the same solutions? Is one approach likely to be more accurate than another?

Note: This task is adapted from one developed by Marge Petit, when she was a middle school teacher at Cabot School, Cabot, Vermont, and published by *Exemplars*, RR 1, P.O. Box 7390, Underhill, VT 05489.

SCORING GUIDE

	Level One	Level Two	Level Three	Level Four
Mathematical Accuracy and Reasonableness	Inappropriate operation(s) selected, and/or many errors, leading to wildly erroneous conclusions.	Some errors evident in either operations selected, computations, or sense of reasonableness.	Appropriate operation(s) selected; few or no errors; with reasonable results.	Computational accuracy and evidence of flexibility in evaluating reasonableness.
Approach	Random and disorganized; no systematic approach.	Some system apparent in the approach, but not well organized.	Systematic and organized single approach.	Highly systematic and organized approach, verified through another.
Explanation	Little or no explanation given.	Explanation attempted, but difficult to understand.	Explanation fairly clear, but thinking process not always easy to follow.	Explanation very clear, and thinking process easy to follow.

SAMPLES OF STUDENT WORK

LEVEL ONE

The lady put the popcorn in a scale with cups. and then we put some stuff in the other side We did it because we thought it would work and it did. but first we were doing something els with the popcorn we were puting it on a ruler then we stoped that.

We did not
we used the skail to hold it.

This response reveals little or no understanding of the problem nor a systematic approach to solving it.

We had a scale and som wates and popcorn crnls. We tuck a 5 gm and put it on one side and then we put the pop corn crnls in on the other side and wade it till it was perfict. Then we made little pills and counted them. They all ecwold up to 55.

This response, while stronger than the one above, demonstrates no coherent approach to the problem. The student appears to be still at the stage in the problem of exploring with the materials.

LEVEL TWO

The problem was to estimate How many popcorn Kernels there were in the container. We had these items to help us figure out or estimate: a Scale three sizes of cups; a calculater; a ruler; and some graph paper.

at frist we did not Know what to do the we decided to make some measurements to help us whith the actual estimale. We figured out that 1 tile weighed the same as 52 popcorn Kernels. based on that we did our frist estimation we Just multiplied 52 x 52   becase that Looks good up there our answer was 2074 wich   Later became a very good answer   for we had two other estimates   within 400 of it, but the other one was a bit high.

The way we got it was by Counting the amount of Kernels there were in one midixm cup wich was 256 then we multipled the wumber of cups there were in the container wich was twelve our answer was 3072 a little higher than the other three estimates.

This response demonstrates understanding of the problem and appears to have been based on three different approaches to the problem. However, the explanation is difficult to follow and the computations are not clearly described.

LEVEL THREE

We have another problem in Math in class. We have to estimate how many Popcorn kernels are in a big container by using tiny cups, big cups, weight scale, and a calculator.

The first way we thought of to solve the problem was to pour the Popcorn into the scale so that there's exactly half in each side then we would count half. That way would take forever, so we found another way. Here's how we did it. We counted how many kernels fit in a little cup, exactly 246. Then we counted how little cups fit into big cups, 6. We had four big cups and 1 and a half little filled with Popcorn kernels. Then we multiplied 246 by 24 plus the extra popcorn and came up with our estimation of 6261. kernels. When I really think about it. The first way I tried to solve the problem wouldn't of taken so long if I devided the kernels into fourths and counted them I could have solved the problem two ways.

This response demonstrates a systematic approach to the problem and contains the hint of a second method that could have been used for verification. The explanation is clear and the computations are accurate and reasonable.

LEVEL FOUR

The problem is to estimate how many popcorn kernels there are in a big container.

I wasn't quite sure if I was going to like this problem. In the end it turned out to be an okay problem.

How we figured it out was like this: We decided that we should figure out how many kernels would fit in a small cup. Because then we would be able to say when we filled up a small cup there are about somany kernels in this cup. There were 243 kernels.

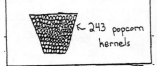

← 243 popcorn kernels

So we filled the small cups then put the kernels into a bigger cup. Three of the small cups fit in the big cups.

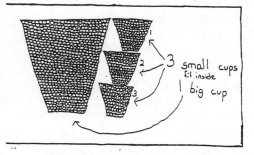

3 small cups fit inside
1 big cup

So we punched 243 into the calculator each time we filled a tiny cup. But in the end we ended up with 532,170 popcorn kernels! We knew that sounded kind of wrong so we decided to check our answer. We knew that three of the little cups filled with popcorn kernels fit

LEVEL FOUR (CONTINUED)

into one big cup. There were five
big cups and one little cup so
there were 16 little cups total. (see last page)
Then we took the calculator and
pressed in 16×243. The answer
came out to be 3,888. So my
group had two totally different
answers. We didn't know which
one was right! We decided to
check one more time. This time we
wrote 243 16 times on a peice
of paper. When we added it all
up it was 3,888.
    So our final answer is
3,888.
    Out of this problem I
learned that the next time I
use a calculator I need to
be very careful that I press
the numbers I want so I don't
end up with a totally wild
answer!
    I will use estimation in
my job when I grow up. Lets
say I became an artest.
I would estimate how much
paint I would need to finish
that picture and I would
estimate how long it would
take me to finish the picture.

The explanation in this solution is clear and easy to follow. Its
author has a keen sense of the reasonableness of results, and
the group had to re-do one of their estimates because of wild-
ly different results. However, the response is a weak "four"
because it demonstrates essentially only one approach to the
problem.

SKYDIVING

MATHEMATICS STANDARDS ASSESSED

- Geometry and measurement
- Problem solving and mathematical reasoning
- Mathematical skills and tools
- Mathematical communication

DIRECTIONS TO THE STUDENT

Miss Stewart (a teacher in the school) is planning to go skydiving. She wants to surprise Miss Bucci and land on her farm. However, she would prefer to land on open area rather than on a building or in the pond. Using the aerial photograph of the farm in the space below, determine the probability that Miss Stewart will land in part of the open area of the farm.

Explain in words how you arrived at your answer.

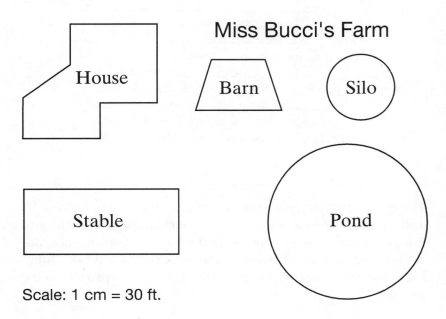

Miss Bucci's Farm

House

Barn

Silo

Stable

Pond

Scale: 1 cm = 30 ft.

MATHEMATICAL CONCEPTS

This task requires that students apply skills of measurement and calculation to a semi-authentic situation. They must measure correctly, calculate areas of different shapes, and then calculate the percentage of land covered by buildings or the pond and subtract from 1.00.

SOLUTION

The area of open farmland is approximately 85%.

SCORING GUIDE

	Level One	Level Two	Level Three	Level Four
Mathematical Accuracy	Inappropriate operation(s) selected, and/or many errors, leading to wildly erroneous conclusions.	Mixture of appropriate and inappropriate operation((s); some errors, but allowing largely for accurate conclusions.	Appropriate operation(s) selected; virtually no mathematical errors; with accurate conclusions.	In addition, the work shows evidence of advanced planning.
Approach	Random and disorganized; no systematic approach.	Some system apparent in the approach; however, it is difficult to follow.	Systematic and organized approach, but not well presented.	Highly systematic and organized approach; neatly and clearly presented.
Explanation	Little or no explanation, or impossible to follow.	Explanation attempted, but difficult to understand.	Explanation fairly clear, but thinking process not always easy to follow..	Explanation very clear, and thinking process easy to follow.

This task was developed by Donna Bucci, eighth grade teacher in the Penn Delco School District, Ashton, PA.

SPOT

MATHEMATICS STANDARDS ASSESSED

- Number operations and concepts
- Functions and algebra
- Problem solving and mathematical reasoning
- Mathematical skills and tools
- Mathematical communication

DIRECTIONS TO THE STUDENT

Each month John weighs his puppy Spot, with the results shown below. If the pattern of the puppy's weight gain continues, how much will he weigh at 5 months? How much do you think Spot will weigh when he is fully grown?

Explain how you arrived at your answers.

Spot's Age	Spot's Weight
1 month	10 lbs.
2 months	15 lbs.
3 months	19 lbs.
4 months	22 lbs.
5 months	?

MATHEMATICAL CONCEPTS

In this task, students must analyze the data provided to determine the pattern shown there. They must then extrapolate to determine the age at which Spot will not gain more weight.

This task is adapted from one developed for the National Assessment of Educational Progress (NAEP).

SOLUTION

This task, unlike many performance tasks, has a single right answer. The pattern in the weight gain is a gain of one less pound per month. That is, between months one and two, Spot gained 5 pounds, but only 4 pounds between months two and three, and 3 pounds between months three and four. The pattern is illustrated in the table below:

Spot's Age	Spot's Weight	Weight Gain
1 month	10 lbs	-
2 months	15 lbs	5 lbs
3 months	19 lbs	4 lbs
4 months	22 lbs	3 lbs
5 months	24 lbs	2 lbs
6 months	25 lbs	1 lb
7 months	25 lbs	0 lb

Continuing the pattern, Spot would gain 2 pounds between months four and five, weighing 24 pounds at five months. Then, Spot would gain 1 additional pound between months five and six, but then gain no more weight. Therefore, he would have gained all his weight by the time he is six months old.

SCORING GUIDE

	Level One	Level Two	Level Three	Level Four
Pattern Recognition and Extension	No awareness of the pattern	Recognition that there is a pattern, but incorrect conclusion as to what it is.	Correct recognition of pattern but inability to extend.	Correct recognition and extension of pattern.
Explanation	No or wholly inadequate explanation provided	Explanation unclear	Explanation clear.	Explanation very clear and well articulated.

TRAFFIC LIGHTS

MATHEMATICS STANDARDS ASSESSED

- Statistics and probability
- Problem solving and mathematical reasoning
- Mathematical skills and tools
- Mathematical communication

DIRECTIONS TO THE STUDENT

It often seems as though traffic lights are always red! Sometimes, though, you can be lucky, and ride through a whole series of lights that turn green just as you approach them.

Imagine you are on a bus, riding along a stretch of road with five traffic lights. They are timed to allow them the same amount of time for each of the two roads in the intersection. What are the chances that all the lights will be red when your bus gets to them? What are the chances that they will all be green?

Write an explanation of how you arrived at your answer.

MATHEMATICAL CONCEPTS

This task requires students to apply concepts of probability to a practical situation they are likely to encounter frequently.

SOLUTION

This problem, unlike many performance tasks, has a single correct answer.

Since the problem states that the lights are timed so that both roads of the intersection have the same amount of time devoted to them, the likelihood of any one light being red (or green) is 50%. Therefore, the likelihood of all the lights being red (or green) when a person reaches it is $1/2 \times 1/2 \times 1/2 \times 1/2 \times 1/2$ or $1/32$.

Some students might try to solve the problem by adding the probabilities of each of the individual events, rather than multiplying them.

Scoring Guide

	Level One	Level Two	Level Three	Level Four
Computational Accuracy	Major computational errors, reflecting little understanding of the mathematical concepts.	Problem not set up correctly; but few computational errors given the manner in which the problem is set up.	Problem set up correctly; only minor computational errors.	No errors, and the problem is set up correctly.
Explanation	Explanation reveals little understanding of the concepts of probability.	Explanation difficult to follow, and reveals only partial understanding of the concepts of probability.	Explanation adequately reveals understanding of the concepts of probability.	In addition, the explanation is very clear and succinct.

TV SHOW

MATHEMATICS STANDARDS ASSESSED

- Functions and algebra
- Statistics and probability
- Problem solving and mathematical reasoning
- Mathematical skills and tools
- Mathematical communication

DIRECTIONS TO THE STUDENT

You have been asked by a TV producer to make recommendations about a new show. The TV station has decided they want to create a weekly show (with advertisers) that will appeal to middle school students, and they need your help. What type of shows do you and your friends like? What type of show do you think your friends would watch?

Devise a method of answering this question, and write a letter to the TV producer with your recommendations. You might consider:

- Designing and conducting a survey of students in your school.

- Organizing and analyzing the information you receive from the surveys.

- Determining whether the preferences of students in your school are typical of all middle school students.

- Preparing a visual representation of the information in a table, graph, or chart.

- Drawing conclusions from the types of shows students like and making your recommendations to the TV producer.

MATHEMATICAL CONCEPTS

In this task, students must apply concepts of sampling, survey design, and data analysis to a practical situation. They must also organize the data they receive, analyzing the shows that students watch according to pertinent categories. Lastly, they must communicate their findings to a non-technical audience.

SOLUTION

Solutions will vary, according to the students' findings. However, all successful answers will have a well-designed survey instrument, a large sample, some method of extrapolating from the sample to the larger population, organization and analysis of the data, a method of presenting the information in visual form, and a coherent narrative explaining the findings.

SCORING GUIDE

	Level One	Level Two	Level Three	Level Four
Design of Survey Instrument	Questions very limited; will not serve to obtain necessary information.	Questions will elicit almost all information required for the task.	Questions will elicit all information required	In addition, questions asked in a manner to ease later data analysis.
Analysis of Data	Data poorly organized; hard to read and interpret.	Data organization is uneven; categories not well conceived.	Data well organized but presented in a haphazard manner.	Data well organized and neatly presented.
Quality of Graph	Graph seriously flawed: inappropriate type, inaccurate, or error in execution.	Graph has one serious error	Graph is appropriate to the data, and is accurate.	In addition, the graph is well presented, with all details well executed.
Letter to Producer	Ideas are not accurately summarized; a producer could not act on the findings.	Minor errors in the interpretation of findings.	Interpretation of data essentially accurate; data support findings.	In addition, the findings are presented in an imaginative manner.

VARIABLE DILEMMA

MATHEMATICS STANDARDS ASSESSED

- Number operations and concepts
- Problem solving and mathematical reasoning
- Mathematical skills and tools
- Mathematical communication

DIRECTIONS TO THE STUDENT

Each letter in the equations below stands for a different number (0-9). Look at each equation carefully. Think about what you know about how numbers work. Find the value of each letter (A-J).

Write a brief summary of how you found your answer. It need not describe every step, but should enable a reader to understand your approach.

1. $G + G + G = D$
2. $J + E = J$
3. $G^2 = D$
4. $B + G = D$
5. $F - B = C$
6. $I / H = A$ (H>A)
7. $A \times C = A$

MATHEMATICAL CONCEPTS

This assessment task requires that students apply what they know about properties of numbers (such as the identity and zero principles of addition and multiplication) to solve the problem. In addition, they must be able to suspend judgment until they have sufficient information on which to reach a conclusion and try out different solutions. Lastly, they must be able to communicate their findings and the procedure they have used.

SOLUTION

One possible solution is the following:

A = 2	F = 7
B = 6	G = 3
C = 1	H = 4
D = 9	I = 8
E = 0	J = 5

A possible procedure is as follows:

- Equations #1 and #3 can be combined to conclude that G = 3 and D = 9
- From equation #4 and the statement above it can be concluded that B = 6
- From equation #2 we know that E = 0; J can be anything.
- From equation #7 we know that C = 1; A can be anything.
- From equation #5, since C = 1, F = 7
- Using equation #6 and the numbers remaining, I = 8, H = 4 and A = 2
- J must be 5, since it is the only number left, and J can be anything.

Note: This task is adapted from one developed by Anne Rainey in Shelburne, Vermont, with student work from Clare Forseth's class at the Marion Cross School in Norwich, Vermont, and published by *Exemplars*, RR 1, P.O. Box 7390, Underhill, VT 05489.

SCORING GUIDE

	Level One	Level Two	Level Three	Level Four
Mathematical Accuracy and application of principles of number theory	No findings or few correct answers.	Some recognition of applicability of principles of number theory; some correct answers.	Most answers correct with limited application of principles of number theory.	All answers correct based on complete application of principles of number theory.
Approach	Random and disorganized; no systematic approach.	Some system apparent in the approach, but not well organized.	Moderately systematic approach; some use of trial and error.	Highly systematic and organized approach; no reliance on trial and error.
Explanation	Little or no explanation given.	Explanation attempted, but difficult to understand.	Explanation fairly clear, but thinking process not always easy to follow..	Explanation very clear, and thinking process easy to follow.

SAMPLES OF STUDENT WORK

LEVEL ONE

1) First I looked at problem $J+E=J$. I counted up until I got to J. J is the tenth., letter. So I wrote 10 under the J's. But the problem is addition. So far I had 10 + blank = 10. E must be 0, so that equals: 10+0=10.

2) The next problem I did was F-G=C. G =C, so. F-G=C 7-6=1.)

This response exhibits little awareness of a systematic approach to the problem and provides little explanation.

LEVEL TWO

$$6A = 4 \quad 6I = 2$$
$$4B = 6 \quad 7J = 7$$
$$1C = 1$$
$$4D = 9$$
$$2E = 0$$
$$5F = 5$$
$$3G = 3$$
$$7H - 8$$

(continued on next page)

LEVEL TWO (CONTINUED)

The first letter I got
was C which = 1 because
any thing times 1 = the same number.

The second letter I got was
E because anything + zero
equals that mumber

The third letter I got was
6 the way I got it was I
just had to fool around with
other letters and number thats
also how I got the two fourth
letters

The Fith letter I got was
F the way I got it I
just had too think about it

The sixth letters I were
A,H,I the way I got them
were I looked and saw the
numbers I had not used and
then tried it and got the answers

The seventh letter I
got was J because I forgot
abbout it but then I saw
that I had used all the
numbers below 10 and 10+0
=10 and that was the answer.

This response offers a fairly complete explanation of the procedure followed. However, several of the findings are inaccurate, making others inaccurate also. Awareness of the identity
properties of 0 and 1 permit this student to correctly conclude
that C = 1 and E = 0. However, after that point the steps in reasoning break down, making successful solving of the problem
impossible.

Level Three

$2 \times 1 = 2$

C = 1 because A × C = A and I solved first because any number × itself is one. I came up with A = 2 because I tried different numbers with different equations and A had to be 2. Then I did all the other equations and came up with this chart. A = 2 B = 6 C = 1 D = 9 E = 0 F = 7 G = 3 H = 4 I = 8 J = 5.

If the numbers didn't have to equal one through nine, than J could be any number because J only shows up on the paper in one equation and it could be any number. e.g. 20 = J + O = E = 2 = J

This response arrives at a correct solution to the problem, although the explanation is not complete. However, the student appears to understand the problem and applies the relevant principles of number theory correctly.

LEVEL FOUR

First I discored that $O=E$ because $J+E=J$ and I know that in addition any number plus zero is itself. So on my chart (preivos page) I put a check where E met zero and knowing O or E couldn't be anything else I crossed out all the other possdoiltys for zero and E.

Then I saw $A \times C = A$ and I knew that any number times one is its self. So $C=1$.

Then I saw $G^2=D$ and $G+G+G=D$ so I listed all squares under ten $1, 4, 9$ then I thoaght $\sqrt{1}^{1} \sqrt{4}^{2} \sqrt{9}^{3}$ then $1+1+1=3$. $2+2+2=6$ $3+3+3=9$, and I saw $3^2=9$ and $3+3+3=9$ so $G=3$ and $D=9$.

After knowing $3=G$ $D=9$ I saw $B+G=D$ and so I thought $B+3=9$ and figured $B=6$ because $6+3=9$.

Knowing $B=6$ and $C=1$ I saw $F-B=C$ or $F-6=1$ and relized $7-6=1$ $F=7$.

Then I saw $1-H=8$ ($H > A$). I thought A can't be 8 because it has to be less than H, and H can't be 2 because $H > A$. I also relizec $I > H$ because you're diviing I so H wasn't 8 and I wasn't 3. Then after I thoaght for a bit. I came up with $8+4=2$ it was the only possable combanation so $A=2$ $H=4$ and I equaled 8.

It was them that I saw J could only be 5.

This problem reminds me of logic problems because if you set it up in a grid the same rules apply.

(continued on next page)

LEVEL FOUR (CONTINUED)

	A	B	C	D	E	F	G	H	I	J
1	X	X	✓	X	X	X	X	X	X	X
2	✓	X	X	X	X	X	X	X	X	X
3	X	X	X	X	X	X	✓	X	X	X
4	X	X	X	X	X	X	X	✓	X	X
5	X	X	X	X	X	X	X	X	X	✓
6	X	✓	X	X	X	X	X	X	X	X
7	X	X	X	X	X	✓	X	X	X	X
8	X	X	X	X	X	X	X	X	✓	X
9	X	X	X	✓	X	X	X	X	X	X
0	X	X	X	X	✓	X	X	X	X	X

The explanation in this solution is clear and easy to follow. Its author has developed a systematic procedure for keeping track of which numbers have been used. The approach is logical and systematic, yielding a correct solution with a minimum of trial and error.

Appendix

Student Hand-Outs

Please feel free to photocopy the material in this Appendix
and distribute to your students.

ALL IN A DAY

Name _____

Directions:

Make a graph to illustrate how many hours you spend on a typical school day involved in different types of activities. You should think about time sleeping, eating, being in school, doing homework, watching television, being with friends, playing sports, doing hobbies, etc.

You may want to make a table to organize your information, and you will have to select the best type of graph to use: for example, a bar graph, line graph, or circle graph.

In addition, please show all your calculations and write a brief explanation of why you chose the graph you did and your method used in making the graph.

BASKETBALL CAMP

Name _____

Directions:

Kristin won a 7-day scholarship worth $1000 to the Pro Shot Basketball Camp, but she will have to make some decisions about how to spend the money. Round trip travel expenses to the camp are $335 by air or $125 by train. At the camp she must choose between a week of individual instruction at $60. per day or a week of group instruction at $40 per day. Kristin's food and other living expenses are fixed at $45 per day. If she cannot add more money to the scholarship award, what are all the possible choices of travel and instruction plans that Kristin could afford to make?

Decide how you would recommend that Kristin spend her award, and write a brief letter to her explaining your thinking.

BULL'S EYE

Name _____

Directions

The archery target shown below is made of four circles, with radii of 1 foot, 2 feet, 3 feet, and 4 feet, and with points as marked. If you shoot an arrow at random at the target, and it does not miss the target altogether, what is the chance that you will earn a score of 10? What is the chance of earning a 7? a 5? a 3?

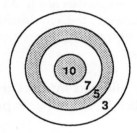

Write an explanation that a younger student could understand, describing how you arrived at your answers.

CHECKERS TOURNAMENT

Name_____

Directions:

Josh, Mike, Stacy, and Carrie have decided to organize a checkers tournament, with themselves as players. If they each play each of the others once only, how many games will be played?

Describe in words the method you used to figure out your answer. You may want to organize your information in a table or make some other "picture" to represent the tournament.

As an extension, determine how many games would have to be played if another student were added to the tournament.

CONCESSION STAND

Name _____

Directions:

You are in charge of scheduling people to work in the concession stand at the state-wide soccer tournament for the next two weekends. Create a schedule that will satisfy the guidelines below, and present it in an organized manner, both to the owner of the stand and to each of the workers.

GUIDELINES

1. The concession stand is open from 9 a.m. to 7 p.m. on the two Saturdays, and from 11 a.m. to 5 p.m. on the two Sundays.

2. There may be one, two, or three people working in the stand at any one time, depending on how busy you think the stand will be.

3. You can pay workers $4.25 per hour; workers should work no more than one shift per day.

4. Your total budget for paying workers for the four days is $350.00, although you don't have to spend it all.

5. If possible, in their different shifts, people should work with different co-workers; every worker does not have to work each day.

Your completed work will include:

• A schedule for the four days (two Saturdays and two Sundays) with the shifts identified, and the number of workers for each shift. For example, you can arrange 1-hour shifts, 2-hour shifts, 3-hour shifts, 4-hour shifts, or some combination of these.

- The number of workers for each shift, reflecting how busy you think the concession stand will be.

- The total number of workers you will need.

- A budget for paying the workers.

- A written description of why you think your schedule is a good one.

COUNTRY MILE

Name _____

Directions:

In an old folk tale, a poor peasant is offered as much land as he can walk around from sunup to sundown. If you were given that offer, how much land could you claim? What shape would it be?

In order to answer these questions, you will have to:

• Determine the length of a day from sunup to sundown. Is it the same every day? At which time of year would you choose to make your walk?

• Determine how fast you can walk in an hour, and how many hours you could walk in the day. You should consider the need for food and rest during the day.

• Determine the best shape to walk around to claim the most land. Will it be a square? Some other rectangle? A circle? Some other shape?

• Calculate the amount of land (in square miles) that you could claim.

Your answer should include:

• Drawings of the different possible shapes you might use, with their respective areas and perimeters,

• A clear presentation of the methods you used to calculate:
- the length of the day
- the distance you can walk
- the area you can claim

• All work should be clearly labeled.

Cover it Up

Name _____

Directions

You are the president of a small painting company that is hoping to win the contract to paint the walls of your math classroom, using two coats of paint. In order to prepare your bid, you need to determine what the paint will cost. Calculate the number of cans of paint that will be needed, and their cost from a store in your area.

In order to find the cost of the paint, you will need to:

• measure and calculate the area of the walls in your math classroom,

• determine how much area a single can of paint will cover, (this is usually stated on the can itself),

• calculate the number of cans required for two coats of paint,

• calculate the amount the paint will cost, and

• describe in words how you found your solution.

You may want to draw a diagram of the classroom. You should show all your work, and present it in a form that is neat and clear to read.

DAYCARE CENTER

Name _____

Directions:

You have been hired by a day care agency to fence in an area to be used for a playground. You have been provided with 60 feet of fencing (in 4-foot sections) and a 4-foot gate. How can you put up the fence so the children have the maximum amount of space in which to play?

1. Try several different shapes that can be made with the fencing and calculate their areas. Make pictures of these shapes, including a scale drawing of the best shape.

2. Write a brief summary that describes which shape you think will have the largest area and why.

3. Imagine that the fencing is flexible, and can be made to bend. What shape would have the greatest area then?

LINEUP

Name _____

Directions:

A baseball team has nine players; the order in which they bat is called the 'batting order' or 'lineup.' For your school's baseball team, how many different lineups are possible? Write a brief description of your reasoning to the coach of the team.

LOCKER COMBINATIONS

Name_____

Directions:

Most school locker combination locks have 30 numbers on their dials, and a series of three numbers (right, left, right) opens the lock. If you forgot your combination, and decided to try all the possible combinations, how many might you have to try? How long do you think it might take you?

Write a brief explanation for your school newspaper explaining how safe you believe combination locks to be.

LUCKY SODA

Name _____

Directions:

A soft drink company has hired you to help organize a promotion for its Cool Mist soft drink by including prizes in some of the bottles. The prizes will be tokens attached to the insides of the lids of the bottles; customers determine whether they have won by scratching the lids.

The soft drink company has created two types of prizes: "gold" awards and "silver" awards; the gold awards are $10.00 coupons for Cool Mist and the silver awards are $2.00 coupons. The company will put the prizes in 500 cases (12 bottles to a case) of soft drinks, and needs a system to decide which bottles to put the winning lids on. They plan to award 25 gold prizes and 250 silver prizes, and need a fair system for distributing them among all the bottles.

On the assembly line in the bottling plant, each bottle is assigned a number. Which bottles should be designated "gold"winners, and which ones "silver" winners so the winning bottles are distributed through the entire 500 cases, and will therefore be distributed around the country? You should be sure that no bottle is assigned more than one prize.

To complete your job for the soft drink company, you should devise a method for awarding the gold and silver prizes such that:

- 25 gold prizes and 250 silver prizes are awarded,
- no bottle has more than one prize
- the prizes are distributed evenly throughout the entire 500 cases.

Write a brief letter to the president of the soft drink company, explaining which bottles should have the gold and silver prizes, and the method you used to designate the winning bottles.

MONEY FROM TRASH

Name _____

Directions:

The eighth grade students at Washington Middle School are trying to raise money to help pay for a class trip. There are 250 students in the class, and they want to raise $2000.00 by recycling newspapers, cans, and glass and plastic bottles. Using the table below, calculate how many pounds of newspaper, cans, and bottles (or different combinations of these) students will have to collect to raise the money.

To complete this task, please:

- Determine how much each student is responsible to raise, and several ways students could fulfill their responsibilities.

- Based on the amount of newspaper, cans, and bottles your own family uses, decide which material you would collect for your contribution.

- Describe in words how you arrived at your conclusions.

MONEY FROM TRASH

Material	Amount per ton
Mixed paper	$40 per ton
Newspaper	$100 per ton
Aluminum cans	$1240 per ton
Steel cans	$50 per ton
Clear glass	$30 per ton
Green glass	-
Amber glass	$15 per ton
Plastic: soda bottles	$240 per ton
Plastic: milk bottles	$300 per ton

MUSIC COMPANY

Name _____

Directions:

A music recording company is trying to decide which groups they should record on their label. They have asked you to help by determining which groups are most popular with students today, and which will be the most popular for several years. They have asked for your recommendations, supported by clear reasons.

In order to complete this job, you might:

- For the students in one of your classes, determine their favorite musical groups, and ones which they think they will like in the next few years. This means that you must design a survey instrument of some kind. It should help you find out:

   - which groups students like now, and

   - which groups students think they will like for the next few years.

- Conduct the survey of students.

- Analyze your data, by organizing it into a table.

- Summarize your findings, by making some type of graph or graphs.

- Calculate how many recordings could be sold to students in your entire school.

- Write a summary to the recording company, in which you recommend to them which artists they should record.

NAME GAME

Name _____

Directions:

A sweatshirt company embroiders names on its sweatshirts; they charge customers for the service. It costs the company $.50 to embroider each letter, and they want to make 100% profit on the service. But they also want to charge a flat fee per name, rather than different amounts for different names. Most people want just their first name on their sweatshirt.

The company has asked you to advise them on the length of first names of young people so they can set a fair price for the embroidered names on the sweatshirts. How long is the average name? What could the company charge for an embroidered name that would enable them to make money overall?

In order to complete this task, you should:

• Determine a method to discover the length of first names,

• Collect and analyze sufficient data to make you confident of your results, and

• Conclude a fair price for the sweatshirt company to charge for embroidering the names.

Write a letter to the president of the company with your recommendation for the price they should charge to embroider people's first names, and the method you used to determine your answer.

OUTFITS

Name _____

Directions:

Maria is going to visit her cousins for the weekend. She packs a pair of purple pants, a pair of jeans, and a pair of blue shorts. For shirts she takes a blue tee-shirt, a white tank top, a yellow blouse, and a green shirt. In addition, she has three pairs of socks: white, yellow, and blue. How many different outfits can she make?

A picture or table will help you to organize the information.

Write a description of how you figured out your answer.

PINHEAD? FAT-HEAD? IN-BETWEEN?

Name _____

Directions:

Do tall people have big heads? How could you find out? Investigate the relationship between height and size of head, and determine whether they are related. Summarize your findings in words and a graph of some kind.

As you decide how to answer this question, you might consider the following steps:

* Select a sample of people. This could be your own class, another class in your school, a group of people in your neighborhood, your soccer team or swim team, or any other group. Think about how large a group you need to draw any conclusions, and whether it matters if they are all students, or a combination of students and adults.

* Measure the height and head circumference of everyone in the group, using appropriate tools.

* Determine whether there is any relationship between height and the size of head, using any method you like.

* Present your findings, through a graph, table, chart, or any suitable approach.

* Write a brief summary of your investigation: how you went about it, what decisions you made and why and what you found. Also include any additional questions you have as a result of your work.

PIZZA PARTY

Name _____

Directions:

Your class has decided to have pizza for its end-of-the-year party. You are trying to decide which pizza store has the cheapest price. The local pizza stores and their prices are listed below.

Pizza Prices

Sam's Pizza House	$8.50, 8 slices per pizza
Pizza Palace	$10.25, 10 slices per pizza
Pizza & Stuff	$6.25, 6 slices per pizza

Assume that there are 30 students in your class, and that each person (including your teacher) will eat two slices. Also assume that the slices in the pizzas from the different stores are the same size. Where should you buy the pizza?

Please show all your work, and write a brief description of how you decided on your answer.

POOL PLEASURE

Name _____

Directions:

Your city Department of Recreation has finally obtained approval for the construction of a swimming pool, and has requested your help with the design, and the timing for filling the pool when it is built.

The pool will have to be able to hold 100 people, and in order for it not to be too crowded, you should allow 20 square feet of surface area per swimmer. The pool should be 3 feet deep in the shallow end, and 9 feet deep in the deep end. You can make the shallow end as large as you like.

What are some possible shapes for the pool? Which do you like best? Which do you think would be the least expensive to build?

When the pool is built, how long will it take to fill? If the Recreation Department wants to open the pool on Memorial Day weekend (May 25), when should they begin filling it? The pipe they will be using can supply water at the rate of 6 gallons per minute, and a cubic foot of water contains 7.48 gallons.

Draw a picture of your pool, and write a letter to the Director of Recreation to explain your recommendations.

POPCORN ESTIMATION

Name _____

Directions:

Estimate how many popcorn kernels there are in the container. You may use any of the materials in the classroom, including graph paper, scales, cups, rulers, calculators.

Be sure to explain your strategy and your reasoning. Think how you might verify your estimate.

<u>Materials Needed</u>

- A large jar filled with popcorn kernels
- Cups of several different sizes, such as portion cups from a hospital, 7 oz cold drink cups
- Scales or pan balance and weights (standard or non-standard)
- Graph paper
- Calculators

SKYDIVING

Name _____

Directions:

Miss Stewart (a teacher in the school) is planning to go skydiving. She wants to surprise Miss Bucci and land on her farm. However, she would prefer to land on open area than on a building or in the pond. Using the aerial photograph of the farm in the space below, determine the probability that Miss Stewart will land in part of the open area of the farm.

Explain in words how you arrived at your answer.

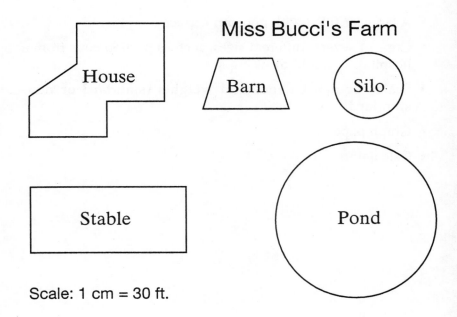

Miss Bucci's Farm

House

Barn

Silo

Stable

Pond

Scale: 1 cm = 30 ft.

SPOT

Name _____

Directions:

Each month John weighs his puppy Spot, with the results shown below. If the pattern of the puppy's weight gain continues, how much will he weigh at 5 months. How much do you think Spot will weigh when he is full grown?

Explain how you arrived at your answers.

Spot's Age	Spot's Weight
1 month	10 lbs.
2 months	15 lbs.
3 months	19 lbs.
4 months	22 lbs.
5 months	?

TRAFFIC LIGHTS

Name _____

Directions:

It often seems as though traffic lights are always red! Sometimes, though, you can be lucky, and ride through a whole series of lights that turn green just as you approach them.

Imagine you are on a bus, riding along a stretch of road with five traffic lights. They are timed to allow them same amount of time for each of the two roads in the intersection. What are the chances that all the lights will be red when your bus get to them? What are the chances that they will all be green?

Write an explanation of how you arrived at your answer.

TV SHOW

Name _____

Directions:

You have been asked by a TV producer to make recommendations about a new show. The TV station has decided they want to create a weekly show (with advertisers) that will appeal to middle school students, and they need your help. What type of shows do you and your friends like? What type of show do you think they would watch?

- Devise a method of answering this question, and write a letter to the TV producer with your recommendations. You might consider:

- Designing and conducting a survey of students in your school.

- Organizing and analyzing the information you receive from the surveys.

- Determining whether the preferences of students in your school are typical of all middle school students.

- Preparing a visual representation of the information, in a table, graph, or chart.

- Drawing conclusions from the types of shows students like to your recommendations to the TV producer.

VARIABLE DILEMMA

Name _____

Directions:

Each letter in the equations below stands for a different number (0-9). Look at each equation carefully. Think about what you know about how numbers work. Find the value of each letter (A-J).

Write a brief summary of how you found your answer. It need not describe every step, but should enable a reader to understand your approach.

$G + G + G = D$
$J + E = J$
$G^2 = D$
$B + G = D$
$F - B = C$
$I/H = A$ (H>A)
$A \times C = A$